Unit Assessment

Bothell, WA • Chicago, IL • Columbus, OH • New York, NY

www.mheonline.com/readingwonders

Send all inquiries to:
McGraw-Hill Education
Two Penn Plaza
New York, New York 10121

Printed in the United States of America.

4 5 6 7 8 9 QMD 17 16 15 14 13
C

The McGraw-Hill Companies

Table of Contents

Unit Assessment

Unit Assessment is an integral part of the complete assessment program aligned with ***McGraw-Hill Reading Wonders*** and the Common Core State Standards (CCSS).

Purpose of *Unit Assessment*

Unit Assessment reports on the outcome of student learning. As students complete each unit of the reading program, they will be assessed on their understanding of key instructional content. The results of ***Unit Assessment*** serve as a summative assessment by providing a status of current achievement in relation to student progress through the CCSS-aligned curriculum. The results of the assessments can be used to inform subsequent instruction, aid in making leveling and grouping decisions, and point toward areas in need of reteaching or remediation.

Focus of *Unit Assessment*

Unit Assessment focuses on key areas of English Language Arts as identified by the CCSS—comprehension of literature and informational text, vocabulary acquisition and use, command of the conventions of the English language, and writing within the parameters of specific text types.

Administering *Unit Assessment*

Each unit assessment should be administered once the instruction for the specific unit is completed. Make copies of the unit assessment for the class. You will need one copy of the Answer Key page that features the scoring table for each student taking the assessment. This table provides a place to list student scores. The data from each unit assessment charts student progress and underscores strengths and weaknesses.

NOTE: Due to time constraints, you may wish to administer the unit assessment over multiple days. For example, students can complete Questions 1–40 on the first day and address the writing prompt on another. If you decide to break-up administration by assessment sections, please remember to withhold those sections of the test students are not completing to ensure test validity.

After each student has a copy of the assessment, provide a version of the following directions:

Say: *Write your name and the date on the question pages for this assessment.* (When students are finished, continue with the directions.) *In the first part of the test, you will read three selections and answer questions about them. In the next part of the test, you will read drafts and/or passages. You will revise these for clarity or edit for the correct grammar, mechanics, and usage. In the final part of the test, you will read a prompt and write a response. Read each part of the test carefully. For multiple-choice items, completely fill in the circle next to the correct answer. For constructed response items, write your response on the lines provided. For the writing prompt, plan your writing on the lines provided and craft your final version on another sheet of paper. When you have completed the assessment, put your pencil down and turn the pages over. You may begin now.*

Answer procedural questions during the assessment, but do not provide any assistance on the items or selections. Have extra paper on hand for students to use for their responses to the prompt. After the class has completed the assessment, ask students to verify that their names and the date are written on the necessary pages.

Overview of *Unit Assessment*

- Students will read three selections in each assessment and respond to items focusing on Comprehension Skills, Literary Elements, Text Features, and Vocabulary Strategies. These items assess the ability to access meaning from the text and demonstrate understanding of unknown and multiple-meaning words and phrases.
- Students will then read a draft that requires corrections or clarifications to its use of the conventions of English language and/or complete a cloze passage that requires correct usage identification.
- Students are then presented with a writing prompt that asks them to craft a response following the expectations of a particular text type.

Reading Selections

Each unit assessment features three "Cold Read" selections on which the comprehension and vocabulary assessment items are based. These selections reflect the unit theme to support the focus of the classroom instruction. Selections increase in complexity as the school year progresses to mirror the rigor of reading materials students encounter in the classroom.

Comprehension—Multiple-Choice Items

Comprehension items in each unit assess student understanding of the text through the use of the Comprehension Skills, Literary Elements, and Text Features that were the focus of each unit's instruction.

Comprehension—Constructed Response/Performance Task

A total of six items in each unit assess student understanding of the text by having them craft a written response to a question/prompt. Four of the items are short response items that assess student comprehension of the text using Comprehension Skills, Literary Elements, and Text Features. These items feature six lines on which students can write their responses. Two of the items are extended response, performance task items. One item requires student interaction with multiple texts; the other requires focus on a particular text. These items feature a page of lines on which students can write their responses.

Vocabulary—Multiple-Choice Items

Vocabulary items in each unit ask students to demonstrate the ability to uncover the meanings of unknown and multiple-meaning words and phrases using the Vocabulary Strategies that were the focus of each unit's instruction.

English Language Conventions/Grammar, Mechanics, Usage—Multiple-Choice Items

A total of ten items in each unit ask students to demonstrate their command of the conventions of standard English. Students are required to correct errors and clarify writing by editing/revising existing drafts or completing cloze passages.

Writing—Writing Prompt

Students craft a written response to a prompt in a previously-taught text type––Narrative, Informational, or Opinion. This activity assesses students' ability to write on demand in response to a prompt and is consistent with the writing performance students encounter in high-stakes testing. Students use the lines provided to plan their writing and compose their final version on a separate sheet of paper.

Scoring *Unit Assessment*

Questions 1–40 constitute a fifty-point test.

Multiple-choice items are worth one point each; short response items are worth two points; and extended response items are worth four points. For written responses, use the correct response parameters provided in the Answer Key and the scoring rubrics listed below to assign a score. Responses that show a complete lack of understanding or are left blank should be given a *0*.

Short Response Score: 2

The response is well-crafted and concise and shows a thorough understanding of the underlying skill. Appropriate text evidence is used to answer the question.

Short Response Score: 1

The response shows partial understanding of the underlying skill. Text evidence is featured, though examples are too general.

Extended Response Score: 4

- The student understands the question/prompt and responds suitably using the appropriate text evidence from the selection or selections.
- The response is an acceptably complete answer to the question/prompt.
- The organization of the response is meaningful.
- The response stays on-topic; ideas are linked to one another with effective transitions.
- The response has correct spelling, grammar, usage, and mechanics.

Extended Response Score: 3

- The student understands the question/prompt and responds suitably using the appropriate text evidence from the selection or selections.
- The response is a somewhat complete answer to the question/prompt.
- The organization of the response is somewhat meaningful.
- The response maintains focus; ideas are linked to one another.
- The response has occasional errors in spelling, grammar, usage, and mechanics.

Extended Response Score: 2

- The student has partial understanding of the question/prompt and uses some text evidence.
- The response is an incomplete answer to the question/prompt.
- The organization of the response is weak.
- The writing is careless; contains extraneous information and ineffective transitions.
- The response requires effort to read easily.
- The response has noticeable errors in spelling, grammar, usage, and mechanics.

Extended Response Score: 1

- The student has minimal understanding of the question/prompt and uses little to no appropriate text evidence.
- The response is a barely acceptable answer to the question/prompt.
- The response lacks organization.
- The writing is erratic with little focus; ideas are not connected to each other.
- The response is difficult to follow.
- The response has frequent errors in spelling, grammar, usage, and mechanics.

Scoring *Unit Assessment*

The Writing Prompt should be scored using the rubric found below.

4-Point Scoring Rubric

	Focus	Organization	Support	Conventions
4	Consistent focus is maintained throughout the writing.	Writing employs an appropriate organizational strategy that is followed throughout.	Writing is clearly supported by specific details. The word choice is precise and engaging.	Writing contains few, if any, errors in the conventions of standard English.
3	Consistent focus is maintained for the most part.	Writing employs an organizational strategy, with occasional digressions.	Writing has supporting details and the word choice serves the purpose of the writing but is not very precise.	Writing contains some errors in the conventions of standard English.
2	Writing loses focus at times.	Writing attempts to use an organizational strategy but it is not clear or consistent.	Writing has few supporting details and the word choice is often simple or unclear.	Writing contains several errors in the conventions of standard English.
1	Writing does not have a consistent focus.	Writing has no organizational strategy.	Writing has a lack of supporting details and the word choice is limited.	Writing contains serious errors in the conventions of standard English.

Unscorable responses are unrelated to the topic, illegible, or contain little or no writing.

Evaluating *Unit Assessment* Scores

The goal of each unit assessment is to evaluate student mastery of previously-taught material. The expectation is for students to score 80% or higher on the assessment as a whole. Within this score, the expectation is for students

- to correctly answer more than 9 of the multiple-choice comprehension items;
- to score "2" on short response items and "3" or higher on extended response items;
- to correctly answer more than 7 of the multiple-choice vocabulary items;
- to correctly answer more than 7 of the multiple-choice items assessing conventions of standard English; and
- to score "3" or higher on their written response to the prompt using the 4-Point Rubric.

For students who do not meet these benchmarks, assign appropriate lessons from the Tier 2 online PDFs. Refer to the unit "Summative Assessment" spreads in the Teacher's Editions of ***McGraw-Hill Reading Wonders*** for specific lessons.

The Answer Keys in ***Unit Assessment*** have been constructed to provide the information you need to aid your understanding of student performance, as well as individualized instructional and intervention needs.

This column lists the instructional content from the unit that is assessed in each item.

Question	Answer	Content Focus	CCSS	Complexity

This column lists the CCSS alignment for each assessment item.

This column lists the Depth of Knowledge associated with each item.

23	B	Main Idea and Key Details	RI.4.2	DOK 2
24	I	Context Clues	L.4.4a	DOK 2
25	A	Prefix *re-*	L.4.4b	DOK 1
26	see below	Main Idea and Key Details	RI.4.2	DOK 2

Correct answer parameters for the constructed response items are found after the scoring table.

Comprehension: Multiple-Choice 1, 6, 8, 12, 14, 16–19, 21, 24–26, 28	/14	%
Comprehension: Constructed Response 9, 10, 20, 23, 29, 30	/16	%
Vocabulary 2–5, 7, 11, 13, 15, 22, 27	/10	%
Grammar, Mechanics, Usage 31–40	/10	%
Total Unit Assessment Score	/50	%

Scoring rows identify items by assessment focus and item type and allow for quick record keeping.

Read the next two articles. Then answer the questions that follow them.

Communicating Coast to Coast

In 1850, the United States Congress passed a bill making California the thirty-first state. It took nine weeks for the news to reach California. Today, news like that would zoom across the country in an instant.

Traveling to the West

Gold was discovered in California in 1848. This caused many Americans to head west in search of fortunes. We call it the "gold rush," but no one got there quickly. The cheapest way to travel west was by covered wagon. It was also the slowest. A wagon trip from St. Louis, Missouri took about six months.

Some people traveled by sea. Ships sailed around South America. The trip from New York City to San Francisco was more than 16,000 miles. One ship made the trip in 89 days in 1851, but people wanted faster ways to travel. More importantly, they wanted faster ways to send information.

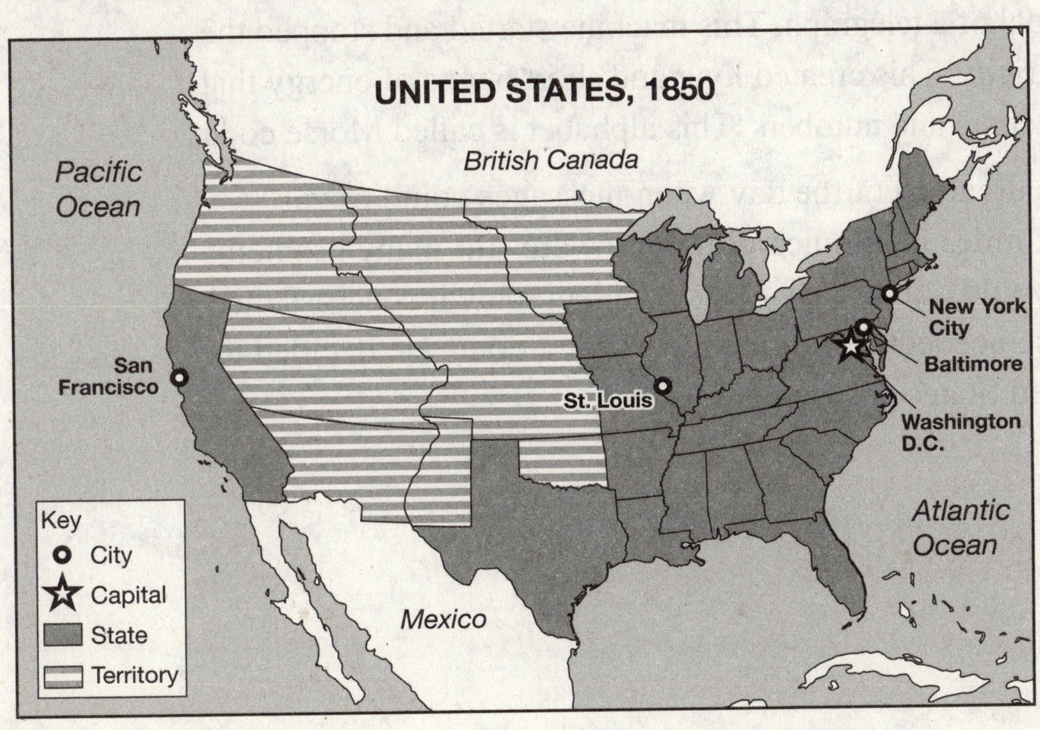

GO ON →

Carrying the Mail

In 1858, stagecoaches began carrying mail. Letters traveled from St. Louis to San Francisco in just 25 days. Soon the mail traveled even faster when carried on horseback. The Pony Express was a series of stations across the West. Riders on horseback carried a pouch of mail from one station to the next. The first rider handed the mail pouch to the next rider, who rode off at great speed. At the next station, the pouch was handed off again, and so on until it reached the final station.

The Pony Express helped information travel more quickly. However, a revolutionary change in the way messages traveled was already taking place. A man named Samuel Morse was leading the way.

Connecting East and West

Morse overheard people discussing whether it would be possible to send messages along a wire. The idea excited him. He knew electricity traveled along a wire in an instant. Imagine sending messages that way!

His inventive mind got right to work. Morse soon had a working model of a telegraph. This machine started and stopped the flow of electricity. This created long and short bursts of energy that represented letters and numbers. This alphabet is called Morse code.

Morse dreamed of the day when messages could travel thousands of miles in minutes. But there were still many problems to solve. It would not be easy to string telegraph wires across the nation. Morse needed a lot of money to get it done. He decided to ask the United States government for help.

GO ON →

When Morse first presented his idea to Congress, they thought his idea seemed impossible. Eventually, Congress gave Morse enough money to get started. He demonstrated how the telegraph worked by sending a message from Baltimore, Maryland, to Washington, D.C. It worked! Those who had made fun of him were convinced. They regretted having ridiculed him.

Connecting the nation from coast to coast by telegraph was a big job. Finally, in 1861, wires from the East joined wires from the West and the transcontinental telegraph was complete! As soon as the telegraph reached completely across the continent, news traveled at lightning speed. This led to the end of the Pony Express because even the fastest horses were no match for the telegraph.

Into the Future

Most telegraph messages were short. Because telegraph offices were not located in every town, many people still sent family news through the mail. Still, the telegraph paved the way for today's high-speed world of telephones, cell phones, text messages, television, radio, and the Internet.

GO ON →

Theodore Judah and the Road West

During the 1850s, many people believed that a railroad could not be built across the United States. They claimed the mountains and deserts of the West could not be crossed. Theodore Judah, however, was sure the job could be done.

Judah was an American railroad engineer who dreamed of the first transcontinental railroad. Judah studied engineering in college. After working on several railroads in the Northeast, he was hired to work for a railroad in California.

He continued to focus on his dream of connecting the East and West. He was sometimes called "Crazy Judah" because of this dream. But he was determined to reach his goal. As the chief engineer of the Central Pacific Railroad, he began laying tracks eastward from California. Tracks for the Union Pacific Railroad were being laid from the East at the same time. The plan was to join the tracks somewhere in the middle of the country. This would form the transcontinental railroad.

The Difficult Path Ahead

Building the Central Pacific Railroad was a challenge. Lying directly in the railroad's path were the Sierra Nevada. These mountains had cliffs sharp as knives that dropped without warning into steep canyons. If Judah and his crew were going to succeed, they had to figure out how to lay tracks through this rugged territory. Workers were lowered over cliffs in baskets. They used hammers to carve paths into the sides of the mountains. Then these paths were widened enough to lay railroad tracks. It was slow work.

GO ON →

Judah and his crew faced many obstacles. During the first winter, the wind piled snow 50 feet high. Wooden snow sheds were built to protect the workers and the tracks. Even with this protection, there were problems. Workers suffered from frostbite. Judah often ordered these workers to be sent back to California for treatment.

Snow sheds allowed work to continue throughout the winter.

The slowest work was digging Summit Tunnel. Day and night, hammers and chisels bit into the rock. Even though the men worked constantly, they only removed about two inches of rock a day. It was the most expensive quarter-mile of railroad track in history.

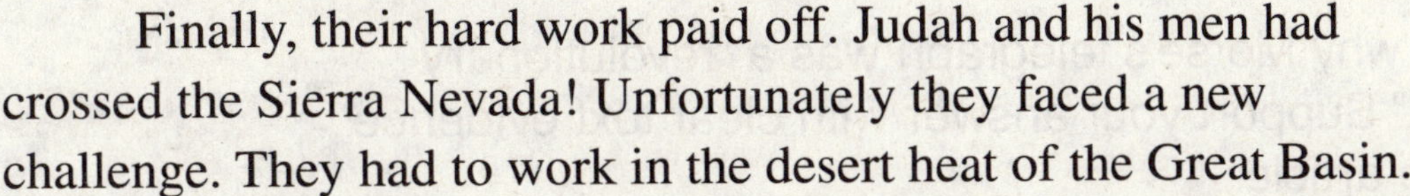

Finally, their hard work paid off. Judah and his men had crossed the Sierra Nevada! Unfortunately they faced a new challenge. They had to work in the desert heat of the Great Basin.

Even with all these difficulties, the Central Pacific Railroad joined the Union Pacific Railroad in 1869. At Promontory, Utah, a crowd of people were thrilled to see a golden spike driven into the tracks to mark the special occasion. Unfortunately, Theodore Judah died before the railroad was completed, but he and many other brave people proved it could be done.

GO ON →

Name: ______________________________ Date: ________

Use "Communicating Coast to Coast" on pages 1 through 3 to answer Numbers 1 through 10.

1. The author compares and contrasts the Pony Express and telegraph to show the reader

   Ⓐ how technology changed over time.

   Ⓑ the difference in how much each cost.

   Ⓒ why people preferred to use the telegraph.

   Ⓓ that the telegraph was an easier way to communicate.

2. What is the MAIN idea of the article?

   Ⓕ There were many ways to go west during the gold rush.

   Ⓖ Ways to communicate became faster after 1850.

   Ⓗ It took a long time for news to travel West in 1850.

   Ⓘ The telegraph put an end to the Pony Express.

3. Explain why Morse's telegraph was a "revolutionary change." Support your answer with clear text evidence from the article.

   ____

   ____

   ____

   ____

   ____

   ____

GO ON →

Name: ______________________________ Date: __________

4 Read these sentences from the article.

His inventive mind got right to work. Morse soon had a working model of a telegraph.

If *invent* means "to create something for the first time," what does *inventive* mean?

Ⓕ having the ability to invent

Ⓖ someone who invents

Ⓗ the act of inventing

Ⓘ being invented

5 Which was the FASTEST way to send information from St. Louis to California during the late 1850s?

Ⓐ clipper ship

Ⓑ stagecoach

Ⓒ pony express

Ⓓ covered wagon

6 Read this sentence from the article.

This led to the end of the Pony Express because even the fastest horses were no match for the telegraph.

Which meaning of *match* is the SAME one used in the sentence above?

Ⓕ a narrow strip of wood or cardboard used to light a fire

Ⓖ a person viewed as a possible marriage partner

Ⓗ a thing that is equal in quality or strength

Ⓘ a pair of things that appear to be alike

GO ON →

Name: ______________________________ Date: __________

7 Read these sentences from the article.

Those who had made fun of him were convinced. They regretted having ridiculed him.

What does *ridiculed* mean in the sentences above?

Ⓐ punished

Ⓑ instructed

Ⓒ agreed with

Ⓓ made fun of

8 What information can you find in the article under the heading "Connecting East and West"?

Ⓕ ways to travel to California

Ⓖ how the telegraph was built

Ⓗ how the Pony Express worked

Ⓘ reasons for moving to California

9 According to the article, how did Morse convince Congress that the telegraph was a good idea?

Ⓐ He explained his plan to them.

Ⓑ Wires from east and west were joined.

Ⓒ He sent a message from one city to another.

Ⓓ He used a special code for sending messages.

GO ON →

Name: ______________________________ Date: __________

10 Explain how the author uses cause and effect to help the reader understand how communication changed over time. Support your answer with clear text evidence from the article.

GO ON →

Name: ______________________ Date: ________

Use "Theodore Judah and the Road West" on pages 3 and 4 to answer Numbers 11 through 20.

11 Which of these details MOST likely explains why Judah was hired to work on the transcontinental railroad?

Ⓐ He studied engineering in school.

Ⓑ He was born in Bridgeport, Connecticut.

Ⓒ He was sometimes called "Crazy Judah."

Ⓓ He began laying tracks eastward from California.

12 Read this sentence from the article.

> **These mountains had cliffs sharp as knives that dropped without warning into steep canyons.**

Which meaning of the word *steep* is the SAME one used in the sentence above?

Ⓕ too high or unreasonable

Ⓖ to soak or leave in liquid

Ⓗ to involve or absorb deeply

Ⓘ having a very sharp face or slope

13 Read this sentence from the article.

> **As the chief engineer of the Central Pacific Railroad, he began laying train tracks eastward from California.**

The suffix *-ward* means "in the direction of." What does *eastward* mean?

Ⓐ looking like the east

Ⓑ toward the east

Ⓒ full of the east

Ⓓ like the east

GO ON →

Name: ______________________ Date: ________

14 Read this sentence from the article.

Building the Central Pacific Railroad was a challenge.

Which detail from the article does NOT support this idea?

Ⓕ Workers suffered from frostbite.

Ⓖ Workers were lowered over the cliffs in baskets.

Ⓗ He began laying tracks eastward from California.

Ⓘ During the first winter, the wind piled snow 50 feet high.

15 Read this sentence from the article.

Judah was an American railroad engineer who dreamed of the first transcontinental railroad.

Which of the following key details supports this idea?

Ⓐ The plan was to join the tracks somewhere in the middle of the country.

Ⓑ He was the chief engineer of the Central Pacific Railroad.

Ⓒ Building the Central Pacific Railroad was a challenge.

Ⓓ But he was determined to reach his goal.

16 Why did Judah order some workers to go back to California during the first winter?

Ⓕ They needed treatment for frostbite.

Ⓖ They had crossed the Sierra Nevada.

Ⓗ They could not work because of the snow.

Ⓘ They only removed two inches of rock a day.

GO ON →

Name: ______________________________ Date: __________

17 What "huge challenge" did Judah and his men face near the end of the project?

Ⓐ Workers were lowered in baskets over the cliffs.

Ⓑ Hammers and chisels bit into the rock day and night.

Ⓒ They had to lay tracks in the desert heat of the Great Basin.

Ⓓ Tracks for the Union Pacific Railroad were being laid from the East.

18 Read these sentences from the article.

Judah and his crew faced many obstacles. During the first winter, the wind piled snow into drifts 50 feet high.

Which word means almost the SAME as *obstacles*?

Ⓕ challenges

Ⓖ meetings

Ⓗ opportunities

Ⓘ temperatures

19 Use clear text evidence and details to explain why Theodore Judah was called "Crazy Judah."

____

____

____

____

____

____

GO ON →

Name: ______________________________ Date: ________

Use "Communicating Then and Now" and "Theodore Judah and the Road West" to answer the question below.

20 Samuel Morse and Theodore Judah were innovators. This means they created something new or found a new way to do something. Use clear text evidence and details to explain how these individuals did something innovative.

____

____

____

____

____

____

____

____

____

____

____

____

____

____

____

____

GO ON →

Read the passage "The Kitchen Boy and the Prince" before answering Numbers 21 through 30.

The Kitchen Boy and the Prince

Once upon a time, there lived a very dissatisfied prince. He always lost interest in what he had and wanted something else. Nothing pleased him for very long.

Hoping to solve the problem, a wizard gave the prince a marvelous little gadget. It played songs and told stories at the touch of a button. Now, the prince was instantly entertained.

Unfortunately, the problem only got worse. Now the prince stayed in his room staring at his fabulous gadget all day. The more he used it, the less patience he had for anything else. When servants brought food, the prince yelled, "Take it away. Bring me something I like!"

The prince's behavior threw the kitchen staff into a tizzy. They began to panic. Day after day, they worked to create the most pleasing delicacies imaginable. Day after day, the prince looked up from his gadget and rejected the tasty foods they offered.

"This is driving me up the wall," announced the head cook. "There's no pleasing him. I quit!"

The king and queen grew worried. They made a grand announcement of a reward to any person who could help their son find his appetite again. Chefs throughout the land lined up to offer their finest meals. One after another, they left in disgrace. There was no pleasing the prince.

A boy named Nassem worked in the castle kitchen. He walked to work each morning through the beautiful woods and fields that surrounded the castle. Everyday he carried a chunk of bread and a vegetable or fruit to eat for breakfast. He also filled his pockets with nuts and berries he picked along the way.

GO ON →

"The prince is strange," he thought. To Naseem, food always tasted wonderful. As he thought about how good it was to eat after his long walk to work, a plan began to form in his mind. Naseem asked to see the king and queen.

"What?" they exclaimed. "A kitchen boy dares try his luck?" The king and queen thought of all the chefs that had tried and failed. Finally, they decided to give Naseem a chance.

The next day Naseem stood in the prince's room. "Where is your food," the prince demanded. "I must take you to the food, Your Highness," Naseem replied.

The prince grumbled and complained. He did not want to stop using his gadget. But at last he agreed to go at the queen's urging.

Naseem led the prince on a long walk. They climbed hills and crossed streams. The sun shone on them, and a soft breeze blew. Gradually, the prince lost his grumpy scowl. He ran with Naseem and even leaped a fence. When they got to the cottage where Naseem lived, the prince flopped on the grass in exhaustion. Naseem picked an apple from a tree and gave it to the prince. The prince took a big bite.

"What have you done to make this apple taste so good?" asked the prince.

"You've done it, Your Highness," Naseem answered.

The prince devoured the apple. Next Naseem gave him some fresh bread and a drink of cold spring water to complete the meal. "Nothing has ever tasted better," declared the prince.

From that day forth, Naseem became an official companion to the prince. Every Wednesday, Naseem and the prince went outside for exercise and fresh air, no matter what the weather. The prince complained less and less. And he never stopped marveling at how delicious his food always tasted on Wednesdays!

GO ON →

Name: ______________________________ Date: ________

Now answer Numbers 21 through 30. Base your answers on the passage "The Kitchen Boy and the Prince."

21 Which of the following is the solution to the prince's problem?

Ⓐ Chefs offer their finest meals.

Ⓑ The wizard gives the prince the gadget.

Ⓒ The king and queen announce a reward.

Ⓓ Outdoor exercise gives the prince a good appetite.

22 The wizard hoped his gadget would solve the prince's problem. Instead it created new problems. On the lines below, list three problems that the gadget created. Support your answer with clear text evidence from the passage.

____

____

____

____

____

____

GO ON →

Name: ______________________ Date: ________

23 Read these sentence from the passage.

The prince's behavior threw the kitchen staff into a tizzy. They began to panic.

What does the idiom *into a tizzy* mean in the sentences above?

Ⓐ made them nervous

Ⓑ put them in a locked room

Ⓒ forced them to work harder

Ⓓ helped them feel proud of their work

24 Read these sentences from the passage.

Day after day, they worked to create the most pleasing delicacies imaginable. Day after day, the prince looked up from his gadget and rejected the tasty foods they offered.

What does *delicacies* mean in the sentences above?

Ⓕ gadgets

Ⓖ workers

Ⓗ hot spices

Ⓘ tasty foods

25 What does the prince do AFTER he gets the new gadget but BEFORE he walks with Naseem?

Ⓐ eats fresh bread and butter

Ⓑ refuses to eat the foods people offer

Ⓒ asks Naseem why the apple tastes so good

Ⓓ enjoys the delicious taste of food on Wednesdays

GO ON →

Name: ______________________ Date: ________

26 What does Naseem do FIRST in the passage?

Ⓕ talks to the prince

Ⓖ forms a plan in his mind

Ⓗ talks to the king and queen

Ⓘ carries his breakfast to work

27 Read these sentences from the passage.

"This is driving me up the wall," announced the head cook. "There's no pleasing him. I quit!"

What does the idiom *driving me up the wall* mean?

Ⓐ hurting me

Ⓑ making me crazy

Ⓒ trying to please me

Ⓓ locking me in a room

28 Read these sentences from the passage.

The prince devoured the apple. Naseem gave him some fresh bread and a drink of cold spring water to complete the meal. "Nothing has ever tasted better," declared the prince.

Which word has almost the SAME meaning as *devoured*?

Ⓕ ate

Ⓖ grabbed

Ⓗ hid

Ⓘ tossed

29 Which of these events happens LAST in the passage?

Ⓐ The wizard gives the prince a new gadget.

Ⓑ The king and queen offer a reward.

Ⓒ Naseem gives the prince an apple.

Ⓓ The cook says, "I quit."

GO ON →

Name: ______________________ Date: ________

30 Why did Naseem's solution to the prince's problem succeed when others failed? Support your answer with clear text evidence from the passage.

GO ON →

This is the first draft of a story written by Adele. It contains mistakes. Read the story. Then answer Numbers 31 through 40.

(1) Kayla was reading a story to two squirmy twins their names were Jerome and Ella. (2) The story was about a little monkey named Chester. (3) Always getting into trouble.

(4) Jerome and Ella started to giggle. (5) The story was so funny. (6) Kayla just kept on reading. (7) Jerome giggled and squirmed so much that he fell off the bed. (8) Ella gasped, and Kayla stopped reading.

(9) Luckily, the pillows that were usually on the bed. (10) After Jerome got over his surprise, he said, "That was fun!" (11) Everybody laughed. (12) He climbed back up on the bed and rolled off onto the pillows again.

(13) "You are a lot like Chester," said Kayla.

(14) "I'm a monkey!" shouted Jerome. (15) "Monkeys like bananas so do I."

(16) They all went to the kitchen, they found a bunch of bananas in a bowl. (17) "You need to calm down before you can eat," said Kayla. (18) Jerome did not agree. (19) He started to grab a banana Kayla got there first. (20) She held the bowl high in the air. (21) "Close your eyes and count slowly to ten." (22) Jerome calmed down. (23) Ate half a banana before bed.

GO ON →

Name: ______________________ Date: ________

31 Which of these is a run-on sentence?

Ⓐ Sentence 1

Ⓑ Sentence 2

Ⓒ Sentence 3

Ⓓ Sentence 7

32 What is the subject of sentence 2?

Ⓕ Chester

Ⓖ the story

Ⓗ was

Ⓘ a little monkey

33 How can sentence 3 BEST be written?

Ⓐ Chester was always getting into trouble.

Ⓑ Always getting into trouble, which was fun.

Ⓒ Because Chester was always getting into trouble.

Ⓓ Always getting into trouble and enjoying himself.

34 Which is the BEST way to combine sentences 4 and 5 to make a complex sentence?

Ⓕ Jerome and Ella started to giggle, or the story was so funny.

Ⓖ Jerome and Ella started to giggle, and the story was so funny.

Ⓗ Jerome and Ella started to giggle because the story was so funny.

Ⓘ Jerome and Ella started to giggle why the story was so funny.

GO ON →

Name: ______________________ Date: __________

35 Which of these is a compound sentence?

Ⓐ Sentence 6

Ⓑ Sentence 7

Ⓒ Sentence 8

Ⓓ Sentence 9

36 Which sentence contains a subordinate clause?

Ⓕ Sentence 8

Ⓖ Sentence 10

Ⓗ Sentence 11

Ⓘ Sentence 18

37 Which of these is a run-on sentence?

Ⓐ Sentence 7

Ⓑ Sentence 9

Ⓒ Sentence 12

Ⓓ Sentence 19

38 How can sentence 15 BEST be written as a compound sentence?

Ⓕ "Monkeys like bananas, and so do I."

Ⓖ "Because I like bananas so do monkeys."

Ⓗ "Monkeys like bananas before I do."

Ⓘ "Monkeys like bananas, so do I."

GO ON →

Name: ________________________________ Date: ________

39 How can sentence 16 BEST be written as a complex sentence?

Ⓐ They all went to the kitchen, found a bunch of bananas in a bowl.

Ⓑ They all went to the kitchen and found a bunch of bananas in a bowl.

Ⓒ They all went to the kitchen where they found a bunch of bananas in a bowl.

Ⓓ They all went to the kitchen, but they found a bunch of bananas in a bowl.

40 Which of these is a sentence fragment because it does not have a subject?

Ⓕ Sentence 18

Ⓖ Sentence 20

Ⓗ Sentence 22

Ⓘ Sentence 23

STOP

Writing Prompt – Narrative

Everyone has good ideas, and sometimes they pop up at just the right time. Think about an idea you have had in the past. Now write a story about a time when you had a good idea that you shared with a friend or others. Use the space below to plan your writing. Write your story on a separate sheet of paper.

Answer Key

Name: ______________________

Question	Answer	Content Focus	CCSS	Complexity
1	D	Text Structure: Compare and Contrast	RI.4.5	DOK 2
2	G	Main Idea and Key Details	RI.4.2	DOK 2
3	See below	Main Idea and Key Details	RI.4.2	DOK 2
4	F	Suffixes: *-ive*	L.3.4b	DOK 1
5	C	Main Idea and Key Details	RI.4.2	DOK 2
6	H	Context Clues: Multiple-Meaning Words	L.4.4a	DOK 2
7	D	Context Clues: Definitions and Restatements	L.4.4a	DOK 2
8	G	Text Features: Heads and Subheads	RI.4.7	DOK 1
9	C	Cause and Effect	RI.4.5	DOK 2
10	See below	Text Structure: Cause and Effect	RI.4.5	DOK 2
11	A	Cause and Effect	RI.4.5	DOK 2
12	I	Context Clues: Multiple-Meaning Words	L.4.4a	DOK 2
13	B	Suffixes: *-ward*	L.3.4b	DOK 1
14	H	Main Idea and Key Details	RI.4.2	DOK 1
15	A	Main Idea and Key Details	RI.4.2	DOK 1
16	F	Text Structure: Cause and Effect	RI.4.5	DOK 2
17	C	Main Idea and Key Details	RI.4.2	DOK 1
18	F	Context Clues: Synonyms	L.4.5c	DOK 2
19	See below	Main Idea and Key Details	RI.4.2	DOK 2
20	See below	Compare Across Texts	RI.4.9	DOK 2
21	D	Character, Setting, Plot: Problem and Solution	RL.4.3	DOK 2
22	See below	Character, Setting, Plot: Problem and Solution	RL.4.3	DOK 2

Answer Key

Name: ______________________

Question	Answer	Content Focus	CCSS	Complexity
23	A	Figurative Language: Idioms	L.4.5b	DOK 2
24	I	Context Clues: Definitions and Restatements	L.4.4a	DOK 2
25	B	Character, Setting, Plot: Sequence	RL.4.3	DOK 1
26	I	Character, Setting, Plot: Sequence	RL.4.3	DOK 1
27	B	Figurative Language: Idioms	L.4.5b	DOK 2
28	F	Context Clues: Synonyms	L.4.5c	DOK 2
29	C	Character, Setting, Plot: Sequence	RL.4.3	DOK 1
30	See below	Character, Setting, Plot: Problem and Solution	RL.4.3	DOK 3
31	A	Run-on Sentences	L.4.1f	DOK 1
32	G	Subjects and Predicates	L.4.1f	DOK 1
33	A	Sentences	L.4.3b	DOK 1
34	H	Clauses and Complex Sentences	L.4.2c	DOK 2
35	C	Compound Sentences	L.4.2c	DOK 1
36	G	Clauses and Complex Sentences	L.4.2c	DOK 1
37	D	Run-on Sentences	L.4.1f	DOK 1
38	F	Compound Sentences	L.4.2c	DOK 1
39	C	Clauses and Complex Sentences	L.4.2c	DOK 1
40	I	Subjects and Predicates	L.4.1f	DOK 1
Writing Prompt	See below	Narrative Writing	W.4.3a-e	DOK 4

Comprehension: Multiple-Choice 1–2, 5, 8–9, 11, 14–17, 21, 25–26, 29	/14	%
Comprehension: Constructed Response 3, 10, 19, 20, 22, 30	/16	%
Vocabulary 4, 6–7, 12–13, 18, 23–24, 27–28	/10	%
Grammar, Mechanics, Usage 31–40	/10	%
Total Unit Assessment Score	/50	%

Answer Key

Name: ________________________________

3 Responses should include that the telegraph allowed people to communicate from coast to coast in minutes (at lightning speed). Students may mention that Morse also improved existing technologies so they worked better and created his own alphabet for the telegraph.

10 Responses should include how the author uses cause and effect to show how communication changed over time. The author shows that once a form of communication became too slow, a new, faster form came about. For example, people traveled by stagecoach and ships and passed along information by word of mouth or letter. However, with the Pony Express, letters could be sent in a matter of weeks rather than months.

19 Responses should include that many people thought Judah's dream of a railroad that would cross the Sierra Nevada and the Great Basin seemed impossible.

20 **Similarities:** Both wanted to connect the nation from the east coast to the west; both were ridiculed because their dreams seemed impossible; both faced many difficulties; and both met with success. **Differences:** Stringing telegraph lines was not as physically challenging as laying track; Morse was an inventor, while Judah was an engineer; and Morse's project could only send messages, while Judah's could carry people and mail.

22 **Options:** He spent all day staring at the gadget. He had no patience. He refused to eat. The kitchen staff was in a tizzy.

30 Student responses should be in paragraph form and explain that Naseem solved the problem by looking at it in a different way. He helped the prince get hungry instead of giving him different food. Responses should include evidence from the passage to support the idea that Nassem realized fresh air and exercise can make a person hungry or the idea that taking the prince away from the gadget helped him become more active and enjoy life more.

Writing Rubric:

Refer to the scoring criteria in the Teacher Introduction.

Read the article and the passage. Then answer the questions that follow.

How Animals Use Tools

Tools are usually thought of as human inventions. But did you know that animals use tools to solve problems, too?

The chimpanzee, for example, uses grass stems to catch termites. This animal knows where these insects live. It pokes a stem into the termites' nest. Then it waits. Inside the nest, the termites crawl over the stem. The chimpanzee pulls out the termite-covered stem and licks it clean. This is a good meal for a chimpanzee.

Sometimes the chimpanzee has trouble locating water. When this happens, it often uses leaves as a tool. The chimpanzee pushes leaves into places that it cannot reach. The leaves soak up the water from these places. Then the chimpanzee chews on the leaves. Chimps have also been known to use sticks as digging tools.

The woodpecker finch is another animal that uses tools. It uses small sticks to pick insects out of tree bark. Another animal that uses tools is the sea otter. It uses rocks to crack open shellfish. Here is how they do it. The otter places the rock on its chest. Then it holds the shellfish in its paws and bangs it against the rock. This cracks the shell open and allows the otter to eat the creature inside.

This chimpanzee uses a stick as a tool to dig for termites.

GO ON →

The green heron uses bait to catch fish just as humans use bait on the end of a fishing pole. The heron does this by picking up a small object with its beak. It flies over the water and drops the object onto the surface. Beneath the water, fish see the object and swim toward it. The heron waits for fish to swim close to the surface. Then it swoops down and snaps up the fish.

Some animals have uses for tools other than gathering food and water. Some use leaves to dab at wounds or to clean. Some even use twigs as toothpicks. A scientist named Benjamin Beck discovered that crows are very good at solving problems. One unusual crow that lived in Beck's lab ate dry food moistened with a little water. When people forgot to add water to the food, the bird used a cup and added its own water.

The elephant is one of the most intelligent animals. Using its trunk as an arm, the elephant puts grass and branches together. It then uses this tool to swat flies. When needed, this tool can also be used as a back scratcher.

Let's not forget the amazing bottle-nosed dolphins. These remarkable animals twist sea sponges around their snouts. Why? Dolphins hunt the ocean's bottom-dwellers. They use their snouts to turn up sediment and find food. Sometimes they scrape their snouts on sand, rocks, shells, and other objects. Covering their snouts with sponges helps them avoid scrapes, or worse still, stings from poisonous animals.

These are just a few examples of how animals use tools. Scientists are discovering more and more every day. Every time scientists see animals using tools, it makes them rethink their ideas about animal behavior.

GO ON →

Meeting Cody

It was a cool fall day. The air was as crisp as apple cider. Andy was doing exactly what he liked best—racing his bicycle as fast as it would go.

As he sped along the sidewalk, the wind brushed against his face like a cool, refreshing spray. It had been a good day. He gave his report on pandas, and everyone seemed to like it. He scored two goals in the soccer game at recess—life was good.

As he rounded the corner he saw the caution tape and orange cones in front of Mrs. Alemu's house. His Mom warned him to stay away from the hole in the sidewalk. "If you fell in that hole you could be seriously injured. It's best to just steer clear of it altogether," she suggested.

The hole wasn't that deep. Besides, if he was going fast enough surely he could jump it without any problems. It was settled, he would attempt it. He moved the cones onto the grass and headed back to the corner. Andy peddled as fast as he could. He felt like a train thundering down the sidewalk.

As he neared the hole, his mom's warning echoed in his head. Maybe she was right, he might get hurt. "Mom will be really disappointed in me," Andy thought. At the last minute, he changed his mind. Andy suddenly turned onto the grass to avoid the hole. He crashed into the orange cones and fell from his bike.

GO ON →

It had been a week since Andy had broken his leg. He spent all his time lying on the couch or in his room.

"Hey, Andy," his dad said as he walked in the room. "Your buddies are here to see you!" Andy sighed. "Give them a chance," his father said calmly, "they just want to check on you."

As his friends piled through the doorway they could tell Andy was upset, but maybe playing a game would cheer him up. Andy pretended to be tired so the boys just said their goodbyes.

He continued to feel sorry for himself for the next week. Then one day, he woke to something wet on his face. He opened his eyes to a dog staring him in the face. "Surprise!" his parents yelled.

"Great, now the dog can feel sorry for me too," Andy said wiping his cheek with his sleeve.

"Dogs don't feel sorry for people," his father said. "It's people who feel sorry for themselves. We thought adopting this guy would help get you out of this fog you are in."

"Whatever," Andy said without much interest. The dog just sat there, staring at him. "What's his name?" he asked.

"Cody," his mom replied. "We'll let you two get to know each other," she said as they left the room.

After a few minutes Cody nudged Andy's hand with his nose. Andy smiled. Maybe having a dog would be alright. "You want to go out boy?" Andy asked. Cody jumped up excitedly and soon Andy was up too. He hobbled to the back door on his crutches. As they passed through the kitchen Andy's mom whispered, "Well, will you look at that."

As Andy sat on the porch steps he said, "You know, boy, Dad said only people feel sorry for themselves." He paused and leaned down to pick up a stick. "I've spent a lot of time feeling sorry for myself, but that's going to change," he said as he watched Cody chase the stick across the yard.

GO ON →

Name: ______________________ Date: ________

Use "How Animals Use Tools" on pages 28–29 to answer Numbers 1–10.

1 What is the MAIN idea of the article?

Ⓐ The use of tools is a human invention.

Ⓑ Some animals use simple tools to solve problems.

Ⓒ New discoveries make scientists rethink their ideas.

Ⓓ Animals often have problems finding food and water.

2 Which detail shows how the woodpecker finch uses tools?

Ⓕ They use leaves to clean.

Ⓖ They use a stick to catch insects.

Ⓗ They cover their nose to protect it.

Ⓘ They crack shells open with a rock.

3 Read this sentence from the article.

Sometimes the chimpanzee has trouble locating water.

The root word of *locating* suggests that *locating* something means

Ⓐ finding it.

Ⓑ drinking it.

Ⓒ replacing it.

Ⓓ transporting it.

4 Which detail BEST describes how bottle-nosed dolphins use tools?

Ⓕ They often scrape their snouts.

Ⓖ They hunt the ocean's bottom-dwellers.

Ⓗ They use their snouts to turn up sediment.

Ⓘ They wrap sea sponges around their snouts.

GO ON →

Name: ____________________ Date: ________

5 Read this sentence from the article.

Every time scientists see animals using tools, it makes them rethink their ideas about animal behavior.

The prefix *re-* means "again" or it can mean "back" or "backward." Knowing this, what does *rethink* mean?

Ⓐ not think

Ⓑ think again

Ⓒ one who thinks

Ⓓ the act of thinking

6 Explain how the image and caption help you better understand the article. Support your answer with clear evidence from the article.

____

____

____

____

____

____

7 Which sentence BEST summarizes how green herons use tools?

Ⓐ They drop small objects to draw fish to the water's surface.

Ⓑ They use small sticks to get insects out of tree bark.

Ⓒ They use sticks and grass to scratch their backs.

Ⓓ They wrap soft sponges around their beaks.

GO ON →

Name: ______________________________ Date: ________

8 Read this sentence from the article.

> **One unusual crow that lived in Beck's lab ate dry food moistened with a little water.**

The prefix *un-* means "not" or "the opposite of." Something that is *unusual* is

Ⓕ popular.

Ⓖ pretty.

Ⓗ rare.

Ⓘ strong.

9 Which detail BEST supports how an elephant uses tools?

Ⓐ It uses its trunk like an arm.

Ⓑ It uses its trunk to find water.

Ⓒ It uses its intelligence to solve problems.

Ⓓ It uses grass and tree branches to swat flies.

10 Read this sentence from the article.

> **Let's not forget the amazing bottle-nosed dolphins. These remarkable animals twist sea sponges around their snouts.**

Which word means the OPPOSITE of *remarkable*?

Ⓕ boring

Ⓖ dull

Ⓗ ordinary

Ⓘ ugly

GO ON →

Name: ______________________________ Date: ________

Use "Meeting Cody" on pages 30–31 to answer Numbers 11 through 20.

11 How does Andy feel when he considers his mom' s warning about the hole?

Ⓐ angry

Ⓑ embarrassed

Ⓒ impatient

Ⓓ nervous

12 Read this sentence from the passage.

We thought adopting this guy would help get you out of this fog you are in.

What does the metaphor *get you out of this fog* mean?

Ⓕ bring you inside

Ⓖ make you feel better

Ⓗ take you for a walk outside

Ⓘ show you the weather report

13 Read these sentences from the passage.

As he neared the hole, his mom's warning echoed in his head. Maybe she was right, he might get hurt.

What does *echoed* mean as it is used in the sentences above?

Ⓐ to be remembered

Ⓑ to be yelled

Ⓒ to be heard

Ⓓ to be seen

GO ON →

Name: ______________________________ Date: ________

14 Which sentence BEST states the central idea of this passage?

Ⓕ Life is unpredictable.

Ⓖ People can recover from injuries.

Ⓗ Animals don't feel sorry for themselves.

Ⓘ Feeling sorry for yourself will not change a situation.

15 Read these sentences from the passage.

> **Andy peddled as fast as he could. He felt like a train thundering down the sidewalk.**

Find the simile in these sentences. Explain how the two things being compared are related.

____

____

____

____

____

____

16 Who is the narrator of this story?

Ⓕ Andy

Ⓖ Cody

Ⓗ Andy's father

Ⓘ an outside observer

GO ON →

Name: ______________________ Date: ________

17 Read these sentences from the passage.

"If you fell in that hole you could be seriously injured. It's best to just steer clear of it altogether," she suggested.

What do the words *steer clear* mean as used in the sentence above?

Ⓐ direct the movement of

Ⓑ go toward something

Ⓒ control the speed of

Ⓓ stay away from

18 What evidence from the article supports the idea that Andy was a confident, happy kid before the accident?

Ⓕ It was a cool fall day.

Ⓖ The air was as crisp as apple cider.

Ⓗ He continued to feel sorry for himself for the next week.

Ⓘ He scored two goals in the soccer game at recess—life was good.

19 Read this sentence from the passage.

As he rounded the corner he saw the caution tape and orange cones in front of Mrs. Alemu's house.

The root of *caution* means "to be on guard." What does *caution* mean?

Ⓐ be happy

Ⓑ be scared

Ⓒ be warned

Ⓓ be excited

GO ON →

Name: ________________________________ Date: ________

20 Think about the reasons animals use tools in "How Animals Use Tools." The way tools are used in "Meeting Cody" is very different. Contrast the purpose of both sets of tools. Support your answer with clear text evidence from the article and passage. The chart below may help you organize your thoughts.

How Animals Use Tools	Meeting Cody
sticks, pebbles, rocks, grass	cones, bike, crutches, stick

____

____

____

____

____

____

____

____

____

____

____

____

____

GO ON →

Read the poem "Acrobats of the Ocean" before answering Numbers 21 through 30.

Acrobats of the Ocean

The darkened sky recedes at dawn,
Black ocean turns to blue.
A distant sound breaks through the air,
As dolphins come into view.

Like birds on air they rise and jump,
Light dancing off their skin.
They squeak and chatter through the waves,
They leap, they chase, they spin.

They swim as fast as lightning
And protect others in their pod.
Jumping high like shooting stars,
They leave observers awed.

These ballet dancers of the sea
Slap tails, butt heads, and play.
Their curved mouths always smiling,
They look and swim away.

I'd like to be a dolphin,
Taking care of those I love
While dancing in the ocean air,
Sun shining warm above.

GO ON →

Name: ________________________________ Date: __________

21 Read these lines from the poem.

The darkened sky recedes at dawn,
Black ocean turns to blue.

Which word has the OPPOSITE meaning of *recedes*?

Ⓐ advances

Ⓑ lightens

Ⓒ retreats

Ⓓ withdraws

22 You can tell this poem uses first-person narration by

Ⓕ the subject matter of the poem.

Ⓖ the use of the pronoun *I*.

Ⓗ the rhyme scheme.

Ⓘ the use of similes.

23 What is the theme of this poem?

Ⓐ Dolphins need to play.

Ⓑ Dolphins are acrobatic creatures.

Ⓒ The speaker wants to be a dolphin.

Ⓓ Dolphins swim with lightning speed.

24 Who is the speaker in the poem?

Ⓕ a scientist

Ⓖ another dolphin

Ⓗ someone watching dolphins

Ⓘ someone who dances ballet

GO ON →

Name: ______________________________ Date: ________

25 What evidence from the poem supports the speaker's opinion that dolphins are amazing?

Ⓐ They leave observers awed

Ⓑ The darkened sky recedes at dawn

Ⓒ They look and swim away

Ⓓ Sun shining warm above

26 Describe the rhyming pattern in this poem. Support your answer with clear text evidence from the poem.

____

____

____

____

____

____

27 What text evidence from the poem supports the idea that dolphins are active creatures?

Ⓐ They swim as fast as lightning

Ⓑ Their curved mouths always smiling

Ⓒ And protect others in their pod

Ⓓ These ballet dancers of the sea

GO ON →

Name: ______________________________ Date: ________

28 Explain how the comparisons in the poem help the reader understand the speaker's point of view. Support your answer with clear text evidence from the poem.

____

____

____

____

____

____

29 Read these lines from the poem.

Jumping high like shooting stars,
They leave observers awed.

Why does the speaker compare the dolphins to shooting stars?

Ⓐ to show that dolphins are fast swimmers

Ⓑ to suggest that they are an amazing sight

Ⓒ to describe how well dolphins play together

Ⓓ to show the sound dolphins make as they jump

GO ON →

Name: ________________________ Date: ________

30 Use clear text evidence to explain how the speaker feels about dolphins.

GO ON →

Read the passage below. Choose the word or words that correctly complete Numbers 31–35.

I've always loved animals, but we can't have a dog or a cat because my brother is allergic to animal fur. My mother loves animals, too. She works as a volunteer at a local __31__. My __32__ job sounds really fun.

Mom has told me many __33__ about the animals at the shelter. I'm still too young to volunteer, but last week I asked my mom if I could go with her to help. She told me I could but warned me to be ready to work.

__34__ jobs can change every day. Most of the time, Mom helps socialize the cats. This means that she helps cats get used to people so they can be adopted and have better __35__. We spent all afternoon "socializing" the cats.

GO ON →

Name: ______________________ Date: ________

31 Which answer should go in blank (31)?

Ⓐ Animal Shelter

Ⓑ Animal shelter

Ⓒ animal shelter

32 Which answer should go in blank (32)?

Ⓕ mothers

Ⓖ mother's

Ⓗ mothers'

33 Which answer should go in blank (33)?

Ⓐ storys

Ⓑ storyes

Ⓒ stories

34 Which answer should go in blank (34)?

Ⓕ Volunteer's

Ⓖ Volunteers'

Ⓗ Volunteers

35 Which answer should go in blank (35)?

Ⓐ lives

Ⓑ lifes

Ⓒ life

GO ON →

The report below is a first draft written by Miguel. It contains mistakes. Read the report and answer Numbers 36 through 40.

(1) Big cats are large and powerful. (2)They are much bigger and stronger than household cats. (3) Lions cheetahs and leopards are big cats.

(4) Many big cats live in the grasslands of africa. (5)The cheetah is one. (6) It is the world's fastest land mammal. (7) It can run 70 miles per hour. (8) It has excellent eyesight. (9)The cheetah's spotted coat helps it blend into the high grass. (10) It also has long, sharp tooths. (11) Most of the time, the cheetah's prey does not see the cheetah until it is far too late.

GO ON →

Name: ______________________ Date: ________

36 How can sentence 3 BEST be written?

Ⓕ Lions, cheetahs, and leopards are big cats.

Ⓖ Lions cheetahs, and leopards are big cats.

Ⓗ Lions, cheetahs, and, leopards are big cats.

Ⓘ Lions, cheetahs, and leopards, are big cats.

37 How can sentence 4 BEST be written?

Ⓐ Many big cats live in the grasslands of Africa.

Ⓑ Many big cats live in the Grasslands of africa.

Ⓒ Many big cats live in the Grasslands of Africa.

Ⓓ Many big Cats live in the grasslands of africa.

38 How can sentences 5 and 6 BEST be combined as a simple sentence with a subject and a predicate noun?

Ⓕ The cheetah is one, it is the world's fastest land mammal.

Ⓖ The cheetah is one, and it is the world's fastest land mammal.

Ⓗ The cheetah is one, but it is the world's fastest land mammal.

Ⓘ The cheetah is the world's fastest land mammal.

GO ON →

Name: ______________________ Date: ________

39 What is the BEST way to combine sentences 7 and 8?

Ⓐ It can run 70 miles per hour and it has excellent eyesight.

Ⓑ It can run 70 miles per hour, it has excellent eyesight.

Ⓒ It can run 70 miles per hour with excellent eyesight.

Ⓓ It can run and has excellent eyesight at 70 miles per hour.

40 How can sentence 10 BEST be written?

Ⓕ It also has long, sharp tooths.

Ⓖ It also has long, sharp toothes.

Ⓗ It also has long, sharp teeth.

Ⓘ It also has long, sharp teeths.

STOP

Writing Prompt – Informative

Some animals are helpful to people in many ways. Think about an animal that is helpful to people.

Write an informative essay telling about the animal and how it is helpful to people. Use the space below to plan your writing. Write your final copy on a separate sheet of paper.

Answer Key

Name: ______________________

Question	Answer	Content Focus	CCSS	Complexity
1	B	Main Idea and Key Details	RI.4.2	DOK 2
2	G	Main Idea and Key Details	RI.4.2	DOK 1
3	A	Root Words	L.3.4c	DOK 1
4	I	Main Idea and Key Details	RI.4.2	DOK 1
5	B	Prefixes: *re-*	L.4.4b	DOK 1
6	See below	Text Feature: Photos with Captions	RI.4.7	DOK 2
7	A	Main Idea and Key Details	RI.4.2	DOK 1
8	H	Prefixes: *un-*	L.4.4b	DOK 1
9	D	Main Idea and Key Details	RI.4.2	DOK 2
10	H	Context Clues: Antonyms	L.4.5c	DOK 2
11	D	Point of View	RL.4.6	DOK 2
12	G	Figurative Language: Similes and Metaphors	L.4.5a	DOK 2
13	A	Context Clues: Sentence Clues	L.4.4a	DOK 2
14	I	Theme	RL.4.2	DOK 2
15	See below	Figurative Language: Similes and Metaphors	L.4.5a	DOK 2
16	I	Point of View	RL.4.6	DOK 2
17	D	Context Clues: Sentence Clues	L.4.4a	DOK 2
18	I	Theme	RL.4.2	DOK 2
19	D	Root Words	L.3.4c	DOK 1
20	See below	Compare Across Texts	RI.4.9	DOK 4

Answer Key Name: ____________________

Question	Answer	Content Focus	CCSS	Complexity
21	A	Context Clues: Antonyms	L.4.5c	DOK 1
22	G	Point of View	RL.4.6	DOK 1
23	B	Theme	RL.4.2	DOK 2
24	H	Point of View	RL.4.6	DOK 2
25	A	Point of View	RL.4.6	DOK 2
26	See below	Literary Elements: Meter and Rhyme	RL.4.5	DOK 2
27	D	Theme	RL.4.2	DOK 2
28	See below	Theme	RL.4.2	DOK 2
29	B	Point of View	RL.4.6	DOK 2
30	See below	Point of View	RL.4.6	DOK 3
31	C	Common and Proper Nouns	L.4.2a	DOK 1
32	G	Possessive Nouns	L.3.2d	DOK 1
33	C	Singular and Plural Nouns	L.3.1b	DOK 1
34	G	Possessive Nouns	L.3.2d	DOK 1
35	A	Irregular Plural Nouns	L.3.1b	DOK 1
36	F	Singular and Plural Nouns	L.3.1b	DOK 1
37	A	Common and Proper Nouns	L.4.2a	DOK 1
38	I	Combining Sentences	L.4.1f	DOK 2
39	C	Combining Sentences	L.4.1f	DOK 2
40	H	Irregular Plural Nouns	L.3.1b	DOK 1
Writing Prompt	See below	Informative Writing	W.4.2a–e	DOK 3

Comprehension: Multiple-Choice 1–2, 6, 8, 10–11, 14, 16, 18, 22–25, 27, 29	/15	%
Comprehension: Constructed Response 5, 15, 20, 26, 28, 30	/16	%
Vocabulary 3–4, 7, 9, 12–13, 17, 19, 21	/9	%
Grammar, Mechanics, Usage 31–40	/10	%
Total Unit Assessment Score	/50	%

5 Students should explain what they see in the photo and how it helps them understand the article. This photo shows a chimpanzee using a stick as a tool. It shows an example of what the article describes in words.

15 **Simile:** "felt like a train thundering down the sidewalk." Andy is moving, so fast and with such determination to make it to the hole and jump that he feels like a train moving down the tracks full speed ahead.

20 Students should note that people and animals use and need tools to do things they cannot do without help. The animals in the article included: a chimpanzee uses a stick to gather termites and leaves to get water; a woodpecker finch uses a stick to reach bugs; a green heron uses bait to catch fish; an elephant uses grass to swat flies; a bottle-nosed dolphin uses a sponge to protect its snout. **How Animals Use Tools:** The animals use tools for survival; specifically to get food and water. **Cody:** Tools are used to help people move, to warn of dangers, and as toys. Students might infer that animals and people use tools for the other reasons too.

26 Every other line (or the second and fourth lines) in each stanza rhymes ("blue" and "view," "skin" and "spin," etc.). The student may describe this rhyme scheme as abcb.

28 The speaker compares dolphins to birds, to lightning, to shooting stars, and to ballet dancers. These comparisons suggest that dolphins are graceful in their leaping and "dancing," fast-moving, and wonderful to watch.

30 Students should explain that the speaker is fascinated or in awe of dolphins. The speaker explains how they look "like birds on air" and describes how they move in the water. The speaker calls dolphins "ballet dancers of the sea" because they move so gracefully that they appear to be dancing.

Writing Prompt

Refer to the scoring criteria in the Teacher Introduction.

Read the next two articles. Then answer the questions that follow.

John Muir and the Fight for Hetch Hetchy

John Muir and his family came to the United States from Scotland when he was ten years old. He spent much of his life in Wisconsin, but he wanted to explore the West. At the age of 30, Muir arrived in San Francisco. The year was 1868. This was his first visit to California.

He traveled into the mountains known as the Sierra Nevada. The spectacular beauty of the wilderness greatly impressed Muir. He began to spend much of his time exploring and camping there.

Muir loved this land, especially a place known as the Yosemite Valley. In 1870, he began guiding tours in the area. The following year, he visited the Hetch Hetchy Valley. He was surprised to discover a second valley as beautiful as Yosemite! Swift rivers flowed through both valleys. Each was surrounded by towering cliffs. Both valleys were filled with waterfalls, flowering meadows, and ancient forests.

At this time, America was beginning to protect some of its wild places. Yellowstone became the first National Park in 1872. Muir supported the idea of public lands. He began writing and speaking about wilderness conservation. He wrote magazine articles describing the Sierra Nevada, Yosemite, and Hetch Hetchy. In fact, his words helped bring about the creation of Yosemite National Park in 1890.

GO ON →

Hetch Hetchy Reservoir

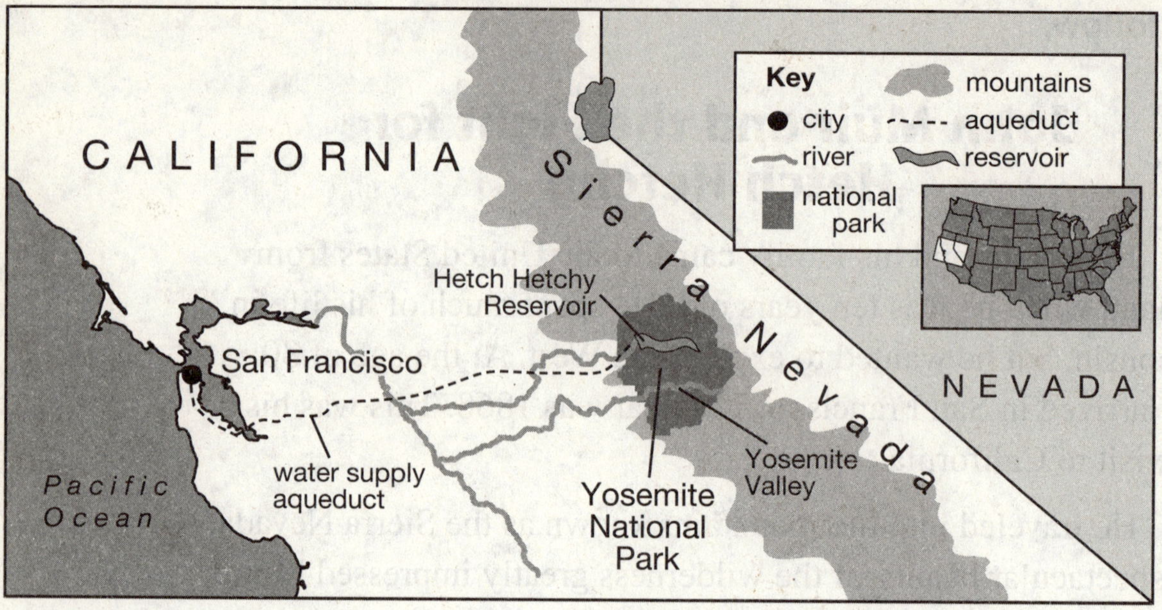

A few years later, Muir met a young man named Gifford Pinchot. Pinchot wanted a career in forestry. Muir was delighted by the young man's interest in the science of managing and caring for forests. He encouraged Pinchot to spend time, not just studying forests, but actually living in them.

Muir became Pinchot's teacher and friend. The two journeyed together through the wilderness. Both men enjoyed living outdoors in all kinds of weather. They both wanted to protect America's forests. Muir and Pinchot agreed that the government should take control of forests and create rules for their use. Otherwise, people wanting to get rich in the mining or lumber industries might destroy America's forests forever.

Muir and Pinchot did not agree on everything. Muir believed in the value of the beauty of nature. He believed that going to the wilderness was good for the body and spirit. He did not believe public lands should be used to make money.

GO ON →

Pinchot believed that it was important to let people profit from public lands. He argued that people could make good use of valuable natural resources, such as water, trees, and grass. He wanted to protect the natural world because it could be useful, with proper management, not because it was beautiful.

In 1901, the city of San Francisco made a plan to put a dam in the Hetch Hetchy Valley. This dam would create a lake that would provide a dependable source of water for the growing city. Muir was horrified. There were other sources of water outside the park that could supply the city's water. He believed it would be wrong to destroy half of Yosemite National Park. Muir did all he could do to stop the project. He created pamphlets and wrote books. He took the President of the United States on a camping trip.

Pinchot, on the other hand, agreed with the people of San Francisco. He believed the dam would provide the greatest good for the greatest number of people. His support was very important in the fight for the dam.

The battle over the dam went on for years. It destroyed the friendship between Muir and Pinchot. Finally, in 1913, San Francisco won the right to build the dam. Sadly, the Hetch Hetchy Valley disappeared forever under a great flood of water.

GO ON →

A Friend of Nature

Rachel Carson grew up on a farm in Pennsylvania. When Carson was a child, she and her dog, Candy, took long walks through the woods near the farm. They looked at the plants and listened to the sounds of birds and animals. Carson's mother encouraged her daughter's curiosity and love of nature. She helped Carson understand that people were a part of nature.

Her mother did a good job. Years later, Carson wanted to learn more about nature. She took classes in biology. She spent many hours walking through forests and fields studying plant and animal life. Before long, Carson knew she wanted to be a scientist.

Carson's work led her to the Massachusetts coast. She had never before seen the ocean. It was so different from the woods and fields of her Pennsylvania childhood. Carson spent many weeks near tide pools. These rocky areas on the edge of the ocean that are filled with seawater. Here she saw unusual creatures she had never observed before. There were starfish in shades of bright red and light pink. Crabs of all sizes, rushed to and fro like scurrying insects.

Carson decided to write a book about the sea. She wanted this book to help people discover the great beauty and the dazzling variety of life sheltered by the ocean. She also wanted people to know that their lives on land depended on the sea. One of Carson's friends was an artist named Bob Hines. He drew many beautiful pictures for this book.

GO ON →

Throughout her life, Carson helped people understand that they should work with nature, not against it. Later, she spoke out against people hurting the environment. She fought against the use of dangerous chemicals that could hurt the enviroment.

One of her books made people aware of how important it is to protect the environment. In the book called *Silent Spring*, Carson warns that if we do not take better care of the environment, we could lose many animals. The title suggests that one day we might have a spring season in which no birds will be heard because they have all died. At the time, some people accused Carson of making a mountain out of a molehill. Today, many people feel that this book started the movement to save the environment.

People did not always agree with Rachel Carson. But she fought for what she believed. In time, more and more people came to understand her point of view.

GO ON →

Name: ______________________________ Date: ________

Use "John Muir and the Fight for Hetch Hetchy" on pages 53–55 to answer Numbers 1–10.

1 The author compares the views of Muir and Pinchot to show the reader

Ⓐ the reasons the dam was a good idea.

Ⓑ arguments for and against the Hetch Hetchy dam.

Ⓒ that California needed water from the dam to drink.

Ⓓ how building the dam would harm the environment.

2 The map is important to the article because it shows

Ⓕ where Hetch Hetchy is located in relation to San Francisco.

Ⓖ how many cities in California use water from national parks.

Ⓗ how many national parks are located in California today.

Ⓘ the location of California's mountain ranges and rivers.

3 Read these sentences from the article.

Pinchot wanted a career in forestry. Muir was delighted by the young man's interest in the science of managing and caring for forests.

What is the meaning of *forestry* in the sentences above?

Ⓐ the business of taking lumber products from forests

Ⓑ the belief that forests are good for body and spirit

Ⓒ the science of managing and caring for forests

Ⓓ the use of forests for recreation and camping

GO ON →

Name: ______________________________ Date: __________

4 The author of the article compares Yosemite Valley to Hetch Hetchy Valley to show

Ⓕ how Hetch Hetchy was first created.

Ⓖ how Muir became friends with Pinchot.

Ⓗ why people travel to see Yosemite today.

Ⓘ why Muir thought Hetch Hetchy was worth saving.

5 How does the author support the point that Muir was upset over the plans for the dam?

____

____

____

____

____

____

6 What evidence does the author use to show that John Muir was an expert in nature? Use details from the article to support your answer.

____

____

____

____

____

____

GO ON →

Name: ______________________________ Date: __________

7. Read this sentence from the article.

He argued that people could make good use of valuable natural resources, such as water, trees, and grass.

What is the meaning of *natural resources* as used in the sentence above?

Ⓐ goods that are made outside

Ⓑ valuable materials placed in nature

Ⓒ making goods through natural processes

Ⓓ materials found in nature that people can use

8. Read this sentence from the article.

He wanted to protect the natural world because it could be useful, with proper management, not because it was beautiful.

What does *management* mean in the sentence above?

Ⓕ bosses

Ⓖ employment

Ⓗ supervision

Ⓘ teaching

GO ON →

Name: ______________________________ Date: ________

9 The people who were pleased with the outcome at Hetch Hetchy would MOST likely agree with which of the following points of view?

Ⓐ When you harm nature, you also harm yourself.

Ⓑ Nature should be used to provide what people need.

Ⓒ Preserving the natural environment is an important goal.

Ⓓ Natural wonders are treasures that people should leave unharmed.

10 What evidence is presented by the author to help the reader understand the fight for Hetch Hetchy?

Ⓕ a comparison of the Hetch Hetchy and Yosemite valleys

Ⓖ arguments for and against the Hetch Hetchy dam

Ⓗ the problems of building the Hetch Hetchy dam

Ⓘ the effects the dam had on San Francisco

GO ON →

Name: ______________________________ Date: __________

Use "A Friend of Nature" on pages 56 through 57 to answer Numbers 11 through 20.

11 Why does the author MOST likely begin this article by telling about Rachel Carson's childhood?

Ⓐ to show that biographies should start at the beginning

Ⓑ to prove that stories about childhood are entertaining

Ⓒ to make a point about how children should be raised

Ⓓ to tell how Carson's childhood influenced her career

12 Read this sentence from the article.

She took classes in biology.

The root of *biology* is the Greek word *bios*, meaning "life." Which word has the same root as *biology*?

Ⓕ botany

Ⓖ biblical

Ⓗ biography

Ⓘ binoculars

13 List three reasons the author considers Rachel Carson to be "a friend of nature."

____

____

____

____

____

____

GO ON →

Name: ______________________________ Date: ________

14 Read this sentence from the article.

Carson's work led her to the Massachusetts coast. She had never before seen the ocean.

Which word has the SAME meaning as ocean?

Ⓕ coast

Ⓖ land

Ⓗ pool

Ⓘ sea

15 What evidence from the text supports the author's opinion that Rachel's mother "did a good job?"

Ⓐ Rachel became a scientist.

Ⓑ Rachel spent many weeks near tide pools.

Ⓒ One of Rachel's friends was the artist Bob Hines.

Ⓓ Rachel's work led her to the Massachusetts coast.

16 Why does the author present Rachel Carson's point of view?

Ⓕ to show what Carson believed

Ⓖ to describe the effects of Carson's work

Ⓗ to tell about the beauty found in tide pools

Ⓘ to explain what causes pollution in the ocean

GO ON →

Name: ______________________________ Date: __________

17 What text evidence supports the author's idea that *Silent Spring* was an important book?

Ⓐ One of her books made people aware of how important it is to protect the environment.

Ⓑ Carson's mother encouraged her daughter's curiosity and love of nature.

Ⓒ People did not always agree with Rachel Carson.

Ⓓ He drew many beautiful pictures for this book.

18 Read these sentences from the article.

There were starfish in shades of bright red and light pink. Crabs of all sizes, rushed to and fro like scurrying insects.

What does *scurrying* mean in the sentences above?

Ⓕ resting quietly

Ⓖ moving rapidly

Ⓗ jumping wildly

Ⓘ swinging slowly

19 Which of these details BEST supports the author's point that Rachel's work was important?

Ⓐ She wrote about the beauty of the ocean and its creatures.

Ⓑ She helped people see their relationship to nature in a new way.

Ⓒ She wanted people to know that life on land is linked to the sea.

Ⓓ She spent hours walking through forests and fields studying life there.

GO ON →

Name: ______________________________ Date: __________

Use "John Muir and the Fight for Hetch Hetchy" and "A Friend of Nature" to answer the question below.

20 How was the work of John Muir and Rachel Carson similar? Explain how the author of each article uses details to explain the importance of their work. Support your answer with clear text evidence from the articles.

GO ON →

Read the passage "Critter Crossing" before answering Numbers 21 through 30.

Critter Crossing

Mr. Singh wants our class to get involved in a community project. He assigned us to small groups to talk about our ideas. Each group needs to come up with an idea for a project to present to the class. Then the whole class will vote to choose a project we can complete together.

I took one look at my group and felt a black cloud of doom overhead. First there was Max. Actually, Max is my friend. But he is completely obsessed with science, which is not really my thing. He got a microscope for his birthday. He thinks it's the most fascinating object in the universe. He can sit at the microscope for hours watching tiny creatures squirm around in a drop of water.

Then there was Iman. All she thinks about is animals. She has a lot of pets at home. Pets are definitely not my thing because I have a lot of allergies.

Finally, there was Cally. She is constantly drawing and sketching. She doesn't talk much. She just sits there and doodles all day, which can be pretty annoying.

As for me, just get me outdoors! That's all I ask.

We sat down to talk about project ideas. As usual, Iman took charge.

"I think we should volunteer at the animal shelter," she said. "It's a great way to help the community, and it will be fun. Of course, that's just one suggestion. I'm going to write down everybody's ideas. But, Theo," she added, staring straight at me, "I really don't think the town needs a new baseball diamond."

How did she know what I was going to suggest?

GO ON →

Then Max spoke up. "What about helping wild animals?" he said. Cally started sketching a tiger on her notepad. "There's a zoologist at the nature center. She has been working to save animals on the road by Warner's Woods. It is causing big problems for the wildlife." He glanced at Cally's notepad. "Sorry, Cally," he said. "I'm talking about amphibians and reptiles. Not that I wouldn't help tigers if I could!"

"So, what are you proposing?" asked Iman.

"Cars and trucks are killing a lot of animals. Spotted salamanders and Blanding's turtles are especially vulnerable. They need to cross the road to get to their nesting grounds. Maybe we could help protect these critters from harm," Max finished.

"We could get the word out so more people know about the problem. We could put signs along the road. They would tell people to watch out for turtles and salamanders," suggested Cally.

"Sure," Max agreed. The zoologist said the spotted salamanders cross the road in huge numbers on the first rainy night in early March. Every year, people from the nature center go out with flashlights and buckets to help them cross safely."

"Maybe some of us could help with that, too," I suggested.

This idea was beginning to sound interesting. We did some research. We found pictures of spotted salamanders and Blanding's turtles. Iman immediately fell in love with them. Cally started designing a "Critter Crossing" sign.

"What we really need is a tunnel under the road," said Max excitedly. "Maybe we could get the town to build one. That's the best way for these critters to cross safely."

Our group of four agreed that Max's Critter Crossing project was a great idea. Now we just have to convince the rest of our class!

GO ON →

Name: ______________________________ Date: ________

Now answer Numbers 21 through 30. Base your answers on "Critter Crossing."

21 Who is the narrator of this passage?

Ⓐ Iman

Ⓑ Max

Ⓒ Mr. Singh

Ⓓ Theo

22 Which of the following opinions would MOST likely come from Cally?

Ⓕ Every family should have at least one pet.

Ⓖ Art is often better than words for expressing ideas.

Ⓗ Studying the world around you is fun and worthwhile.

Ⓘ The school schedule should allow plenty of time for sports.

23 Read this sentence from the passage.

He can sit at the microscope for hours watching tiny creatures squirm around in a drop of water.

The Greek root of *microscope* means "to look at" and *micro* means "small." Based on this, a *microscope* is a tool that is used to

Ⓐ measure time.

Ⓑ cause motion.

Ⓒ test water quality.

Ⓓ view small things.

GO ON →

Name: ______________________________ Date: __________

24 Read these sentences from the passage.

"There's a zoologist at the nature center. She has been working to save animals on the road by Warner's Woods."

A *zoologist* MOST likely works with

Ⓕ animals.

Ⓖ centers.

Ⓗ roads.

Ⓘ woods.

25 What evidence from the text reveals that Iman knows the narrator quite well?

Ⓐ How did she know what I was going to suggest?

Ⓑ "I'm going to write down everybody's ideas."

Ⓒ All she thinks about is animals.

Ⓓ She has a lot of pets at home.

26 Why is the Critter Crossing project a good one from Iman's point of view? Support your answer with clear text evidence from the passage.

____

____

____

____

____

____

GO ON →

Name: ______________________________ Date: ________

27 The narrator would MOST likely put Cally in charge of which part of the project?

Ⓐ making signs

Ⓑ convincing the class

Ⓒ communicating with the public

Ⓓ helping salamanders cross safely

28 Read this sentence from the passage.

"So, what are you proposing?" asked Iman.

Which word has the SAME meaning as *proposing* in this sentence?

Ⓕ announcing

Ⓖ demanding

Ⓗ explaining

Ⓘ suggesting

29 Read these sentences from the passage.

"Spotted salamanders and Blanding's turtles are especially vulnerable. They need to cross the road to get to their nesting grounds. Maybe we could help protect these critters from harm," Max finished.

What does *vulnerable* mean in the sentences above?

Ⓐ hard to find

Ⓑ easy to protect

Ⓒ likely to be harmed

Ⓓ able to take care of themselves

GO ON →

Name: ______________________________ Date: ________

30 Read this sentence from the passage.

I took one look at my group and felt a black cloud of doom overhead.

What does this sentence tell you about the narrator's attitude at the beginning of the passage? Why did the narrator feel that way, and how did those feelings change? Support your answer with clear text evidence from the passage.

____

____

____

____

____

____

____

____

____

____

____

____

____

____

____

____

GO ON →

Read this newsletter article. It is missing some words. Choose the word or words that correctly complete Numbers 31 through 40.

I want to express a big thank-you to everyone who ___(31)___ to the Book Fair last week. The money we earned will buy at least 20 new books for the school library. The Book Fair ___(32)___ a huge success!

Are you ready for some more action? Kayeesha, Noah, and I ___(33)___ the Fall Harvest Festival. The festival will be on November 15. It ___(34)___ a great success in the past. But we'll need a lot of volunteers.

Have you ever ___(35)___ a news announcement? Can you draw? ___(36)___ you good at making posters? If so, we ___(37)___ your talent on the Publicity Team.

Last year, a group of fourth graders ___(38)___ a wonderful puppet show. They performed "The Very Hungry Caterpillar" and ___(39)___ us all a good laugh. We are hoping that some talented actors will plan a performance for this year's festival.

Of course, yummy food is the best part of the Harvest Festival. The pies and spiced cider always ___(40)___ so good! We'll need some great cooks. Please join us as a volunteer and make this year's Fall Harvest Festival the best ever.

GO ON →

Name: ______________________________ Date: ________

31 Which answer should go in blank (31)?

Ⓐ came

Ⓑ comes

Ⓒ was coming

32 Which answer should go in blank (32)?

Ⓕ is

Ⓖ was

Ⓗ will be

33 Which answer should go in blank (33)?

Ⓐ plan

Ⓑ are planning

Ⓒ am planning

34 Which answer should go in blank (34)?

Ⓕ will be

Ⓖ been

Ⓗ has been

35 Which answer should go in blank (35)?

Ⓐ write

Ⓑ wrote

Ⓒ written

GO ON →

Name: ______________________________ Date: ________

36 Which answer should go in blank (36)?

Ⓕ Are

Ⓖ Am

Ⓗ Is

37 Which answer should go in blank (37)?

Ⓐ use

Ⓑ can use

Ⓒ have used

38 Which answer should go in blank (38)?

Ⓕ created

Ⓖ are creating

Ⓗ will create

39 Which answer should go in blank (39)?

Ⓐ give

Ⓑ gave

Ⓒ gived

40 Which answer should go in blank (40)?

Ⓕ tasting

Ⓖ tastes

Ⓗ taste

STOP

Writing Prompt – Persuasive

Everyone has ideas about ways to improve their community. Think about something in your neighborhood or school that you would like to change. How people could work together to make the change happen. Write a speech that will persuade other people to agree with your opinion. Use the space below to plan your writing. Write your speech on a separate sheet of paper.

Answer Key

Name: ______________________

Question	Answer	Content Focus	CCSS	Complexity
1	B	Author's Point of View	RI.4.8	DOK 2
2	F	Text Feature: Map	RI.4.7	DOK 1
3	C	Context Clues: Definitions and Restatements	L.4.4a	DOK 1
4	I	Author's Point of View	RI.4.8	DOK 2
5	See below	Author's Point of View	RI.4.8	DOK 2
6	See below	Author's Point of View	RI.4.8	DOK 2
7	D	Context Clues: Definitions and Restatements	L.4.4a	DOK 2
8	H	Latin and Greek Suffixes: *-ment*	L.4.4b	DOK 2
9	B	Author's Point of View	RI.4.8	DOK 2
10	G	Author's Point of View	RI.4.8	DOK 2
11	D	Author's Point of View	RI.4.8	DOK 2
12	H	Greek Roots	L.4.4b	DOK 2
13	See below	Author's Point of View	RI.4.8	DOK 3
14	I	Context Clues: Synonyms	L.4.5c	DOK 2
15	A	Author's Point of View	RI.4.8	DOK 2
16	F	Author's Point of View	RI.4.8	DOK 2
17	A	Author's Point of View	RI.4.8	DOK 2
18	G	Context Clues: Definitions and Restatements	L.4.4a	DOK 2
19	B	Author's Point of View	RI.4.8	DOK 2
20	See below	Compare Across Texts	RI.4.9	DOK 4
21	D	Point of View	RL.4.6	DOK 1
22	G	Point of View	RL.4.6	DOK 2

Answer Key

Name: ______________________

Question	Answer	Content Focus	CCSS	Complexity
23	D	Greek Roots	L.4.4b	DOK 2
24	F	Latin and Greek Suffixes: *-ist*	L.4.4b	DOK 2
25	A	Point of View	RL.4.6	DOK 2
26	See below	Point of View	RL.4.6	DOK 3
27	A	Point of View	RL.4.6	DOK 2
28	I	Synonyms	L.4.5c	DOK 2
29	C	Context Clues: Paragraph Clues	L.4.4a	DOK 2
30	See below	Point of View	RL.4.6	DOK 3
31	A	Action Verbs	L.3.1d	DOK 1
32	G	Linking Verbs	L.3.1f	DOK 1
33	B	Verb Tenses	L.4.1c	DOK 1
34	H	Main and Helping Verbs	L.4.1c	DOK 1
35	C	Irregular Verbs	L.3.1d	DOK 1
36	F	Linking Verbs	L.3.1f	DOK 1
37	B	Main and Helping Verbs	L.4.1c	DOK 1
38	F	Action Verbs	L.3.1a	DOK 1
39	B	Irregular Verbs	L.3.1a	DOK 1
40	H	Verb Tenses	L.4.1c	DOK 1
Prompt	See below	Persuasive Writing	W.4.1a-d	DOK 3

Comprehension: Multiple Choice 1, 2, 4, 9–11, 15–17, 19, 21–22, 25, 27	/14	%
Comprehension: Constructed Response 5–6, 13, 20, 26, 30	/10	%
Vocabulary 3, 7–8, 12, 14, 18, 23–24, 28–29	/16	%
Grammar, Mechanics, Usage 31–40	/10	%
Total Unit Assessment Score	/50	%

Answer Key

Name: ______________________________

5 The author explains that Muir tried to stop the project by creating pamphlets, writing books, and appealing to the President of the United States.

6 The author includes details about how Muir traveled into the Sierra Nevada and did a lot of exploring and camping.

13 Reasons should include some version of the following ideas. She loved nature and was curious about it; she helped people discover nature's beauty; she helped convince people to take care of the natural environment.

20 Responses should be in paragraph form. Both Muir and Carson worked in and with nature; both loved nature and encouraged others to experience its beauty; both believed it was important to protect nature from people's harmful activities. They were different mainly in where they lived and worked: Muir lived in the mountains of California, and Carson lived by the ocean in Massachusetts. Both authors showed their subjects in a positive light; both also included other points of view, showing that people did not all agree about the importance of protecting the environment.

26 Wording may vary but should include the point that the project involves helping animals. According to the narrator, all Iman thinks about is animals.

30 Student responses should be in paragraph form and should explain that the narrator, Theo, did not think he would enjoy working with the other students in the group. Responses should include Theo's reason for feeling that way, possibly detailing the ways in which members of the group differed from him. Responses should conclude by pointing out that, in the end, Theo was enthusiastic about the project and could see how each member of the group might contribute to it.

Writing Prompt

Refer to the scoring criteria in the Teacher Introduction.

Read the passage and the article. Then answer the questions that follow.

Bessie Coleman and Me

The first time I was in a school play, I felt really uneasy. I was scared that I would make a mistake and people would laugh at me. In the weeks before opening night, I spent a lot of time moping around the house. I nervously went over my lines. I had a great time rehearsing the play with the other cast members, but when I got home, the fear set in. I had a hard time concentrating on my homework, and I could barely eat dinner.

I didn't think anyone noticed what was going on, but apparently my brother Jeremy did. He is a few years older than me. Even though he is usually a real pain, I have to admit that he can be pretty smart sometimes.

One night after dinner, Jeremy saw me in the den, staring blankly at my math book. "What are you doing, Emily?" he asked. "It looks like you are sleeping sitting up."

"I'm studying," I answered, "so leave me alone!"

I must have needed to confide in someone, though, because he ended up getting me to tell him what was going on. I told Jeremy the whole story—the play, my nerves, everything.

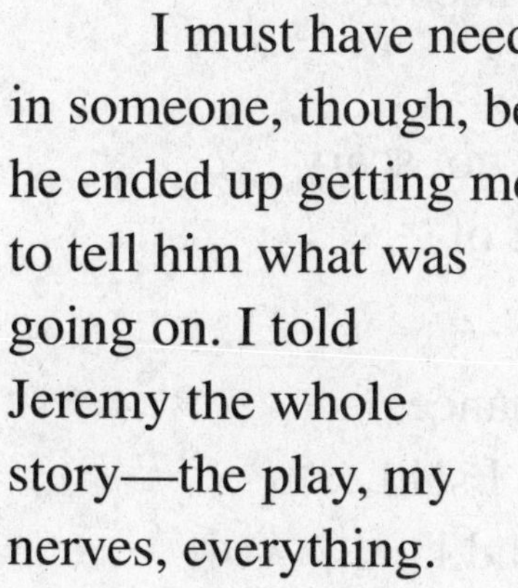

GO ON →

He said, "I just read a really good book about Bessie Coleman. I think you should read it. She was the first African American pilot in the country. She had so many problems to overcome. When she was young, African Americans were not encouraged to become pilots. All Bessie wanted to do was fly a plane. Her family was poor, and she did not go to school full-time. She worked hard, though, and later became a pilot. I think you should read the book."

I was curious, so I took the book and read it right then. Jeremy was right. Bessie Coleman was an incredibly interesting person. When she was young, she took books out of the library and studied them on her own. When she was older, she read all she could about flying. She desperately wanted to be a pilot.

Flight schools in America would not take Bessie because she was African American. So she went to France and learned to fly, and eventually got her pilot's license. She moved back to America with her license and performed in air shows.

After I read this story, I was so inspired! I knew that if Bessie could overcome that many obstacles to become a pilot, and perform in air shows in front of all those people, I didn't need to be afraid of being in a school play!

The opening night of the play turned out to be fun, not scary at all. I felt a few butterflies in my stomach, but I thought of Bessie flying bravely in the sky, and my courage grew.

Many people paid me compliments on my performance, including my brother Jeremy. After he congratulated me, I said these two little words to my big brother: "Thank you." And I secretly thanked Bessie Coleman, too.

GO ON →

Bessie Coleman

Bessie Coleman, 1892–1926

Bessie Coleman was the first African American pilot. There were few ways to earn a living as a pilot in the early days of flight. Bessie built a career as a famous barnstormer. She traveled from town to town performing dangerous stunts in the air.

High Hopes

Bessie was born in Atlanta, Texas on January 26, 1892. She had twelve brothers and sisters. Bessie's family was poor. As Bessie grew older, she helped tend the house and take care of the younger children while her mother worked. Bessie was excited about school and loved to learn. She was especially good at math.

After finishing high school, Bessie left home for college. At that time, flying was a new and exciting adventure. Bessie read about the Wright Brothers and their historic flight at Kitty Hawk in 1903. She also read about Harriet Quimby, a female aviator. Bessie was surprised to learn that a woman could be a pilot. She started to think about flying herself.

In 1915, Bessie moved to Chicago to live near her older brother. She found work, saved her money, and set out to learn to fly. She soon discovered this could never happen in the United States. No flying school would take an African American as a student. If she was going to learn to fly, she was going to have to move to France where schools were more accepting of women and African Americans.

GO ON →

Flying High

In 1920, Bessie arrived in France and began flying lessons. She learned how to take off and how to land. She learned how to bank turns and loop-the-loop. After nearly a year of lessons, Bessie was granted a pilot's license. At the age of 29, she became the first African American to ever earn a pilot's license.

When Bessie arrived home in the United States, she found herself surrounded by reporters. An African American pilot was big news! She told them her dream was to open a flying school that was open to everyone.

Bessie knew her dream was going to cost a lot of money. To earn money she began performing in air shows. This was very dangerous work. Audiences at these shows wanted to see thrilling, perilous stunts. However, Bessie was fearless.

Queen Bess

Bessie performed all kinds of stunts. Often her final stunt was the most exciting. She would fly high up into the sky. Then she turned straight down, pulling out of the dive at the very last moment. Sometimes she flew right over the audience's heads! They applauded loudly. Bessie's popularity grew, and she became a local hero. She was even nicknamed "Queen Bess." Bessie soon began performing all around the country.

On April 30, 1926, Bessie was in Florida preparing for an upcoming air show. She had planned to parachute jump out of the plane for her last exciting stunt. She and her mechanic William Wills took the plane up to practice the stunt. William was in the pilot's seat. During the practice, the plane became unstable and flipped over. Bessie was thrown from the plane before it crashed. Both Bessie and William were killed.

Today, Bessie's spirit of courage and determination still inspires people to meet life's obstacles the way she met her own.

GO ON →

Name: ______________________________ Date: ________

Use "Bessie Coleman and Me" on pages 79 through 80 to answer Numbers 1 through 10.

1. Which sentence from the passage has a first-person point of view.

   Ⓐ I was curious, so I took the book and read it right then.

   Ⓑ All Bessie wanted to do was fly a plane.

   Ⓒ "What are you doing, Emily?" he asked.

   Ⓓ She desperately wanted to be a pilot.

2. What does the first-person point of view help the reader understand in this passage?

   Ⓕ the best way to earn a pilot's license

   Ⓖ how Bessie Coleman still inspires others

   Ⓗ the struggles Bessie Coleman overcame

   Ⓘ why Bessie Coleman did not become a pilot

3. Read this sentence from the passage.

   In the weeks before opening night, I spent a lot of time moping around the house.

   Which word from the sentences above has a negative connotation?

   Ⓐ going

   Ⓑ moping

   Ⓒ opening

   Ⓓ rehearsing

GO ON →

Name: ______________________________ Date: ________

4 Why did Emily find Bessie Coleman's story inspiring?

Ⓕ It gave her the new goal of learning to fly.

Ⓖ It taught her the value of learning about history.

Ⓗ It gave her the courage to perform daring stunts.

Ⓘ It helped her feel ready to overcome her own difficulties.

5 Which sentence BEST states the theme of this passage?

Ⓐ Brothers are often a pain, but they can sometimes be helpful.

Ⓑ Learning about another person's courage can help you feel brave.

Ⓒ Performing in a play can be a challenging and rewarding experience.

Ⓓ Being a pilot was more dangerous in Bessie Coleman's day than now.

6 Describe how Jeremy feels about Emily. Support your answer with clear text evidence from the passage.

____

____

____

____

____

____

GO ON →

Name: ______________________________ Date: ________

7 Describe how Emily felt before the play and how she felt afterward. Support your answer with clear text evidence from the passage.

____

____

____

____

____

____

8 Read this sentence from the passage.

The opening night of the play turned out to be fun, not scary at all. I felt a few butterflies in my stomach, but I thought of Bessie flying bravely in the sky, and my courage grew.

What is the meaning of the idiom *butterflies in my stomach*?

Ⓕ a little nervous

Ⓖ quite confident

Ⓗ having new wings

Ⓘ flying high in the air

GO ON →

Name: ______________________ Date: ________

9 Read this sentence from the passage.

I must have needed to confide in someone, though, because he ended up getting me to tell him how I felt.

The Latin root of *confide* means "trust." Which of these words MOST likely comes from that same Latin root?

Ⓐ confidence

Ⓑ confusion

Ⓒ divide

Ⓓ fierce

10 What evidence from the text BEST supports the theme?

Ⓕ And I secretly thanked Bessie Coleman, too.

Ⓖ She worked hard, though, and later became a pilot.

Ⓗ He said, "I just read a really good book about Bessie Coleman. I think you should read it."

Ⓘ I had a great time rehearsing the play with the other cast members, but when I got home, the fear set in.

GO ON →

Name: ______________________ Date: ________

Use "Bessie Coleman" on pages 81 through 82 to answer Numbers 11 through 20.

11 Which of the following MOST likely caused Bessie to move to France.

Ⓐ Bessie became the first African American to earn a pilot's license.

Ⓑ No flying school would take African American students.

Ⓒ Bessie started to think about flying.

Ⓓ She was especially good at math.

12 Read this paragraph from the article.

Bessie Coleman was the first African American pilot. There were few ways to earn a living as a pilot in the early days of flight. Bessie built a career as a famous barnstormer. She traveled from town to town performing dangerous stunts in the air.

What is the meaning of the word *barnstormer* in this paragraph?

Ⓕ a pilot who performs stunts in air shows

Ⓖ a pilot who has a famous career

Ⓗ a pilot who flies from town to town

Ⓘ a pilot who is African American

GO ON →

Name: ______________________________ Date: ________

13 Why did reporters surround Bessie when she returned from France?

Ⓐ She was going to open a flying school.

Ⓑ She was a famous Frenchwoman.

Ⓒ Her pilot's license was big news.

Ⓓ Her trip to France was big news.

14 Read these sentences from the article.

She also read about Harriet Quimby, a female aviator. Bessie was surprised to learn that a woman could be a pilot.

Which word has almost the SAME meaning as *aviator*?

Ⓕ adventure

Ⓖ flight

Ⓗ pilot

Ⓘ woman

15 Why are the words Queen Bess in boldface type in the article?

Ⓐ They are a nickname.

Ⓑ They draw attention to an unusual fact.

Ⓒ They are a heading for the next section.

Ⓓ They sum up the most important point of the article.

GO ON →

Name: ______________________________ Date: ________

16 Why did Bessie want to earn a lot of money after she returned from France?

Ⓕ She needed to pay a fee for leaving the country.

Ⓖ She needed to pay for her pilot's license.

Ⓗ She wanted to open a flight school.

Ⓘ She wanted to buy a new plane.

17 What evidence from the text BEST explains the cause of Bessie Colman's death?

Ⓐ Bessie performed all kinds of stunts.

Ⓑ Bessie was thrown from the plane before it crashed.

Ⓒ Then she turned straight down, pulling out of the dive at the very last moment.

Ⓓ She had planned to parachute jump out of the plane for her last exciting stunt.

GO ON →

Name: ______________________________ Date: ________

18 Read these sentences from the article.

This was very dangerous work. Audiences at these shows wanted to see thrilling, perilous stunts.

Which word means almost the SAME as *perilous*?

Ⓕ fancy

Ⓗ pretend

Ⓖ magical

Ⓘ risky

19 Read this paragraph from the article.

On April 30, 1926, Bessie was in Florida preparing for an upcoming air show. She had planned to parachute jump out of the plane for her last exciting stunt. She and her mechanic William Wills took the plane up to practice the stunt. William was in the pilot's seat. During the practice, the plane became unstable and flipped over. Bessie was thrown from the plane before it crashed. Both Bessie and William were killed.

What clue from the paragraph helps the reader know what *unstable* means?

Ⓐ William was in the pilot's seat

Ⓑ planned to parachute jump

Ⓒ During the practice

Ⓓ flipped over

GO ON →

Name: ______________________________ Date: ________

Use "Bessie Coleman and Me" and "Bessie Coleman" to answer the question below.

20 Compare how the authors of the passage and article tell the Bessie Coleman story. What is each author's purpose? In what ways are the passages different? Support your answer with clear text evidence from the article and passage.

GO ON →

Read the poem "The Great Road Race" before answering Numbers 21 through 30.

The Great Road Race

by Polly Peterson

Reporter:
A crowd of spectators is gathering here.
They're ready to watch, and they're eager to cheer,
For today is the day of a special road race.
Here come the two runners who'll try for first place.

These two competitors make a strange pair—
A slow, plodding Tortoise and a fast, frisky Hare.
In his colorful outfit, Hare is looking the part.
Wearing only his shell, Tortoise plods toward the start.

Tortoise:
I'll just keep going; it's all I can do.
I know I am slow, but I'm steady, too.

Hare:
Oh, ho—look at me!
I'm as fast as can be!
Today I'm sure to shine,
Victory will be mine.

Mouse:
I'm rooting for Hare,
who is flashy and bright.
I'm betting he'll win,
and I'm sure I'll be right.

I like Tortoise, too—
he's a nice enough guy,
but he can't win the race,
even though he will try.

GO ON →

Reporter:
With a "ready, set, go!" the race has begun.
Hare hops off in a flash—just look at him run!
As everyone knows, Hare is charming and fast,
But his mind often wanders, so his speed may not last.

Tortoise starts slowly; step-by-step he takes off.
He's falling behind, so some people may scoff.
But he sticks to a task, on that you can depend,
His patience may help him to win in the end.

Hare:
Oh, ho—look at me!
I'm as fast as can be!
Today I'm sure to shine,
Victory will be mine.

For me this race will be over in a snap;
I'd still win even if I took a nap.
I can't even see him, he's so far behind.
I'll stop for a snack—the spectators won't mind.

Mmm, look at those carrots, and look at those peas!
I'll eat from this garden as long as I please,
and after I've eaten, I'll lie down to rest.
When I'm feeling tired, I can't run my best.

Reporter:
Hare has fallen asleep, which may not be smart.
When you don't pay attention, your plan falls apart.
And here comes the Tortoise! He's not flashy or fast,
but he seems unwilling to end this race last.

GO ON →

Tortoise:
Oh, me, oh, my, I've traveled a mile,
and I see that Hare has paused for a while.
I'll just keep going; it's all I can do.
I know I'm slow, but I'm steady, too.

Hare:
I've enjoyed a nice rest,
but I'd better get going.
Tortoise might have gone by
without my knowing.

Oh, ho—look at me!
I'm as fast as can be!
Today I'm sure to shine,
Victory will be mine.

Reporter:
Now the great road race is nearing its end.
Here comes the Hare, speeding 'round the bend,
but Tortoise has just stepped over the line—
he got there first! It's his turn to shine!

Mouse:
Wow! Look at Tortoise!
His chances seemed zero,
but he's won the race,
so now he's my hero!

Reporter:
Well, that's it, folks; the race is done.
Hare was favored, but Tortoise won.
Fast and flashy is not always the way;
Sometimes slow and steady wins the day.

GO ON →

Name: ________________________________ Date: ________

Now answer Numbers 21 through 30. Base your answers on "The Great Road Race."

21 Look at the stanzas spoken by the Hare. What is the SAME about all of these stanzas?

Ⓐ the number of lines

Ⓑ the use of repetition

Ⓒ the lengths of the lines

Ⓓ the number of rhyming words

22 Read these lines from the poem.

> **A crowd of spectators is gathering here.**
> **They're ready to watch, and they're eager to cheer,**

The Latin root of *spectators* means "to watch or observe." Which of the following words MOST likely comes from that same Latin root?

Ⓕ expert

Ⓖ inspector

Ⓗ instructor

Ⓘ speaker

23 This poem has four different speakers. Which speaker uses the third-person point of view?

Ⓐ Hare

Ⓑ Mouse

Ⓒ News Reporter

Ⓓ Tortoise

GO ON →

Name: ______________________________ Date: __________

24 Read these lines from the poem.

For me this race will be over in a snap;
I'd still win even if I took a nap.

What is the meaning of the idiom *over in a snap* in these lines?

Ⓕ signing along

Ⓖ being difficult

Ⓗ waiting to start

Ⓘ finished quickly

25 Which word from the poem has a negative connotation?

Ⓐ flashy

Ⓑ frisky

Ⓒ plodding

Ⓓ steady

26 Explain how Mouse's opinion of Tortoise changes at the end the race. Support your answer with clear text evidence from the poem.

____

____

____

____

____

____

GO ON →

Name: ______________________________ Date: ________

27 Which statement or statements by the News Reporter tell the theme of the poem? Support your answer with clear text evidence from the poem.

____

____

____

____

____

____

28 Which of the following is the BEST way to describe Hare?

Ⓕ sure of himself

Ⓖ dependable

Ⓗ patient

Ⓘ tired

29 The author of this poem would MOST likely agree with which of the following themes?

Ⓐ It's foolish to bite off more than you can chew.

Ⓑ Good use of your talents can bring success.

Ⓒ Don't put all your eggs in one basket.

Ⓓ Learn from your mistakes.

GO ON →

Name: ______________________________ Date: __________

30 Two speakers in the poem repeat certain lines. What do the repeated lines tell you about the personalities of the speakers? How do the repeated lines support the poem's theme? Support your answer with clear text evidence from the poem.

____

____

____

____

____

____

____

____

____

____

____

____

____

____

____

____

____

____

GO ON →

Read the story. Choose the words that complete Numbers 31 through 40.

My sister Nita and I don't always agree, but we ____(31)____ alike in one way. We both really like dogs. Terriers and spaniels are my favorite dogs. Chihuahuas are ____(32)____.

We ____(33)____ one big problem, though. Whenever we ask for a dog, our parents simply say, "No pets." They say that ____(34)____ jobs keep them too busy already. They don't want any more responsibilities.

We've tried to convince ____(35)____ that we are old enough to take care of a dog ourselves. We would feed it and walk it and pick up after it. One day we asked again.

"I know ____(36)____ would end up doing most of the work," said Papa. "And I just don't have the time."

"____(37)____ not being fair, Papa!" said Nita. ____(38)____ made her famous pouty face. But Papa didn't change ____(39)____ mind.

So Nita and ____(40)____ have made a plan. To prove that we're ready to take responsibility for a pet, we are starting a dog walking business. Posters advertising our dog-care services are going up tomorrow!

GO ON →

Name: ______________________________ Date: ________

31 Which answer should go in blank (31)?

Ⓐ am

Ⓑ are

Ⓒ is

32 Which answer should go in blank (32)?

Ⓕ hers

Ⓖ his

Ⓗ ours

33 Which answer should go in blank (33)?

Ⓐ are

Ⓑ has

Ⓒ have

34 Which answer should go in blank (34)?

Ⓕ their

Ⓖ there

Ⓗ they're

35 Which answer should go in blank (35)?

Ⓐ their

Ⓑ them

Ⓒ they

GO ON →

Name: ______________________________ Date: ________

36 Which answer should go in blank (36)?

Ⓕ whose

Ⓖ whom

Ⓗ who

37 Which answer should go in blank (37)?

Ⓐ You're

Ⓑ Yours

Ⓒ Your

38 Which answer should go in blank (38)?

Ⓕ He

Ⓖ She

Ⓗ They

39 Which answer should go in blank (39)?

Ⓐ his

Ⓑ her

Ⓒ its

40 Which answer should go in blank (40)?

Ⓕ myself

Ⓖ me

Ⓗ I

STOP

Writing Prompt – Narrative

Sometimes writers treat the same topic in different ways. Think about the story of the Tortoise and the Hare in the poem "The Great Road Race." What do they have in common?

Write a narrative version of this story using two other animals or people. You may change the ending if you wish. Use the space below to plan your writing. Write your story on a separate sheet of paper.

Answer Key Name: ____________

Question	Answer	Content Focus	CCSS	Complexity
1	A	Point of View	RL.4.6	DOK 2
2	G	Point of View	RL.4.6	DOK 2
3	B	Connotation and Denotation	L.4.5	DOK 2
4	I	Point of View	RL.4.6	DOK 2
5	B	Theme	RL.4.2	DOK 3
6	See below	Point of View	RL.4.6	DOK 3
7	See below	Point of View	RL.4.6	DOK 2
8	F	Figurative Language: Idioms	L.4.5b	DOK 2
9	A	Latin Roots	L.4.4b	DOK 1
10	F	Theme	RL.4.2	DOK 2
11	B	Text Structure: Cause and Effect	RI.4.3	DOK 1
12	F	Context Clues: Paragraph Clues	L.4.4a	DOK 2
13	C	Text Structure: Cause and Effect	RI.4.3	DOK 1
14	H	Context Clues: Synonyms	L.4.5c	DOK 2
15	C	Text Features: Boldfaced Words	RI.4.7	DOK 1
16	H	Text Structure: Cause and Effect	RI.4.3	DOK 1
17	B	Text Structure: Cause and Effect	RI.4.3	DOK 1
18	I	Context Clues: Synonyms	L.4.5c	DOK 2
19	D	Context Clues: Paragraph Clues	L.4.4a	DOK 2
20	See below	Compare Across Texts	RI.4.9	DOK 4
21	B	Literary Elements: Stanzas	RL.4.5	DOK 2
22	G	Latin Roots	L.4.4b	DOK 1

Answer Key

Name: ____________________

Question	Answer	Content Focus	CCSS	Complexity
23	C	Point of View	RL.4.6	DOK 2
24	I	Figurative Language: Idioms	L.4.5b	DOK 2
25	C	Connotation and Denotation	L.4.5	DOK 2
26	See below	Point of View	RL.4.6	DOK 3
27	See below	Theme	RL.4.2	DOK 3
28	F	Point of View	RL.4.6	DOK 2
29	B	Theme	RL.4.2	DOK 3
30	See below	Literary Elements: Repetition	RL.4.5	DOK 3
31	B	Pronoun-Verb Agreement	L.3.1f	DOK 1
32	F	Possessive Pronouns	L.3.2d	DOK 1
33	C	Pronoun-Verb Agreement	L.3.1f	DOK 1
34	F	Pronouns and Homophones	L.4.1g	DOK 1
35	B	Types of Pronouns	L.3.1a	DOK 1
36	H	Pronouns and Antecedents	L.4.1a	DOK 1
37	A	Pronouns and Homophones	L.4.1g	DOK 1
38	G	Pronouns and Antecedents	L.4.1a	DOK 1
39	A	Possessive Pronouns	L.3.2d	DOK 1
40	H	Types of Pronouns	L.3.1a	DOK 1
Writing Prompt	See below	Narrative Writing	W.4.3a–e	DOK 3

Comprehension: Multiple-Choice 1–2, 4–5, 10–11, 13, 15–17, 21, 23, 28–29	/14	%
Comprehension: Constructed Response 6, 7, 20, 26, 27, 30	/16	%
Vocabulary 3, 8–9, 12, 14, 18–19, 22, 24–25	/10	%
Grammar, Mechanics, Usage 31–40	/10	%
Total Unit Assessment Score	/50	%

Answer Key Name: ______________________

6 Responses should indicate that Jeremy notices that Emily is worried or uneasy; he gets her to tell him what is wrong and lends her a helpful book; he goes to her performance and congratulates her afterward.

7 Responses should note that before the play, Emily felt restless, worried, fearful, or nervous. She was scared of making a mistake, and "the fear would set in." After the play, she felt happy, grateful, proud, or relieved. She performed well in the play and thanked Jeremy—and Bessie Coleman—for their help.

20 Responses should be in paragraph form and should include ideas similar to the following: The author's purpose in "Bessie Coleman and Me" is to show how Bessie's story could be a source of inspiration. In that story, the fictional character Emily gains courage after reading about Bessie Coleman. The author's purpose in writing the biography of Bessie Coleman is to inform the reader about her struggles, achievements, and death. The passages are different because one is a fictional story and the other is a biography. Both passages tell the story of Bessie Coleman's struggles and achievements, but the biography tells more facts about her life.

26 **Before:** Tortoise is a nice guy, but he can't win. **After:** Tortoise is a hero.

27 Fast and flashy is not always the way; sometimes slow and steady wins the day. *(Accept other statements by the News Reporter that express this theme.)*

30 **Tortoise** He is aware of his strengths and weaknesses. He is humble but determined to do his best. **Hare** He is overly confident with a tendency to brag. **Support of the theme** Sometimes it is better to take an approach that is slow and steady, rather than fast but unreliable.

Writing Prompt

Refer to the scoring criteria in the Teacher Introduction.

Read the article and the passage. Then answer the questions that follow.

Lascaux: A Treasure in the Woods

One night in September 1940, four teen boys headed for the woods near Montignac, a village in France. They were looking for a cave in the woods. The foursome set out to find it with a kerosene lamp and a dog named Robot.

As they entered the woods, Robot ran ahead. The boys hiked along until suddenly, they heard Robot barking. He was in trouble. The boys hurried toward Robot.

The barking was coming from what looked like a rabbit hole. When the boys gathered around to look for Robot, the earth collapsed under them. Shocked, they slid 50 feet down and landed in total darkness.

When 14-year-old Jacques Marsal lit the lamp and looked around, he was awed. There were animals painted all over the walls and ceiling of the cave. The paintings seemed to be moving.

The boys had stumbled into the caves of Lascaux. Inside these caves were some of the most remarkable cave paintings ever found.

Cave Art

These pictures were painted about 17,000 years ago during the Paleolithic Period, which is also called the Stone Age. Nobody knows why these images were painted. But we know the people who created them were highly skilled.

What the Boys Found

The Lascaux caves contain 850 feet of rooms and tunnels. The painted ceilings are as high as 16 feet high.

There are more than 2,000 images of animals, humans, and objects. The animals include horses, stags, bison, and wild oxen. The pictures also show a rhino, a bear, and some big cats. This is amazing because some of these animals do not exist in France today.

GO ON →

The Lascaux painters used different colors to create depth and perspective. They also created some stunning effects by spraying paint onto the walls. Scientists suspect they blew paint through hollow bones, or from their own mouths. With this technique the colors fade together and create shadows. These effects make the animals appear to move.

The artists at Lascaux painted the animals they saw in real life. But creating these paintings was an amazing process. The Lascaux painters had to invent their own tools using the materials of their world. They used bone and plants. They made stone lamps and burned animal fat to create light so they could work in the dark caves.

In order to reach the ceilings, they created structures to stand on that were attached to the walls. To support these structures, they carved holes in the cave walls and attached poles. The structures were then built across the poles. This allowed them to reach the high ceilings.

GO ON →

Hidden Treasure

Jacques Marsal was one of the boys who found the cave in 1940. He never lost that feeling of awe. In fact he devoted his life to protecting the paintings and became Chief Guardian of Lascaux.

When the boys found the caves, the paintings had been hidden for 17,000 years. The air and light in the caves had hardly changed in all those years. The pictures were safe from pollution and changing weather.

After the discovery, the world wanted to see these paintings. The caves were opened to the public in 1948 and received as many as 1,200 visitors per day. Over the next 15 years, exposure to light, fresh air, fungus, temperature changes, and humans began to take a toll. The paintings began to show signs of wear and damage. Officials tried to limit the number of visitors, but that did not work. To protect the paintings and the site, the caves were closed to the public in 1963.

Today, you can see photographs of the cave paintings. You can also visit Lascaux II, which opened in 1983. This is a replica of two halls in the original cave. It was built so that people can see the pictures in a safe way. Only a few experts can visit the caves themselves and see the paintings firsthand.

The paintings of Lascaux are a window to the past. And a picture is worth a thousand words. These paintings tell us a lot about how people lived during the Stone Age, and how they saw the world around them.

GO ON →

Keys to the Past

Jill was feeling discouraged because she had been digging in the Buried City for two weeks. Other students had dug up all kinds of artifacts. All she had discovered was a little metal disc with a man's head on one side but everyone found those.

Suddenly, her trowel hit something in the dirt. She dug quickly, first with the trowel and then with her hands. The object had four sides, each about 15 inches long. The back was about 7 inches high. At the front, there were several rows of flat, shiny buttons. Behind the rows was an array of thin metal rods arranged like a fan with tiny metal heads on the ends. Mounted on the top in the back was a black cylinder. The cylinder had a wheel at both ends and it rotated.

Jill hurried off to Professor Quill's hut. "Sorry, the professor's out. Can you come back in an hour?" The professor's assistant took the artifact and closed the door. Jill returned to the site and continued her digging.

An hour later, Jill watched as the tall, silver-haired Professor Quill and another man studied her artifact. "What do you think, Zap?"

Dr. Zap had pale eyes and wild hair. "These people were hunter-gatherers," he said. "Perhaps they hurled it at animals."

"I don't think so," said the professor. "Look at the symbols on these buttons. They may have believed that touching these symbols would make something magical happen. Remember, this object is at least 4,000 years old and the people who made it were very primitive."

GO ON →

"I doubt— " Dr. Zap began, but the professor interrupted him.

"Very good, Zap!" he said. "Doubt is the beginning, not the end, of wisdom."

Jill coughed politely, and everyone turned to look at her. "I found some more things," she said, holding up a box. The cover was thin and tattered, and hundreds of thin, white sheets were packed inside. Jill removed a single sheet and asked politely, "May I try something?"

The professor nodded. Jill walked over to the artifact. She pushed a button down gently, and one of the metal rods jumped up.

"These buttons are levers," she explained. "That little head on the end of the rod has the same symbol as the button I pressed."

Jill slipped the sheet down behind the cylinder and turned the wheels. The sheet wound itself around the cylinder and came up in front. She pressed one of the buttons, and a rod jumped up. It hit the sheet with a smack. They noticed a black mark appeared on the sheet. It was the same as the symbol on the button she had pressed. One by one, she pushed down the next five buttons in the row. The marks on the sheet looked like this:

qwerty

"Astonishing!" exclaimed Professor Quill.

GO ON →

"This gave me the idea." Jill took a stack of sheets from the box. "These sheets are smaller and they're bound together down the left side. They're nearly covered in the symbols. I think this is a machine that makes symbols, perhaps for communication."

She handed the stack of sheets to the professor. The front and back were hard and shiny. The front showed a picture of a young boy and a one-legged man wearing a three-cornered hat.

Professor Quill opened it. On the first sheet, there were only a few symbols. They looked like this:

TREASURE ISLAND

by

Robert Louis Stevenson

"Remarkable!" said Professor Quill. "You have made an important discovery. We must see if we can figure out what these symbols mean."

GO ON →

Name: ______________________________ Date: __________

Use "Lascaux: A Treasure in the Woods" on pages 106 through 108 to answer Numbers 1 through 10.

1 What happened BEFORE the boys found the cave?

Ⓐ Jacques found a rabbit hole.

Ⓑ They lit a kerosene lamp.

Ⓒ Robot started barking.

Ⓓ They saw a bear.

2 Read this sentence from the article.

> **These pictures were painted about 17,000 years ago during the Paleolithic Period, which is also called the Stone Age.**

The root of *Paleolithic* is the Greek word *paleo*, meaning "old or ancient." Knowing this suggests that *Paleolithic* refers to

Ⓕ older people.

Ⓖ the study of art.

Ⓗ a time long ago.

Ⓘ a place in France.

3 Explain the events that led the boys to find the cave paintings at Lascaux. Support your answer with clear text evidence from the article.

____

____

____

____

____

____

GO ON →

Name: ______________________________ Date: ________

4 How were the painters at Lascaux able to reach the high ceilings?

Ⓕ They sprayed paint through hollowed bones.

Ⓖ They built wooden structures to stand on.

Ⓗ They burned animal fat in stone lanterns.

Ⓘ They made holes in the walls.

5 Read this sentence from the article.

And a picture is worth a thousand words. These paintings tell us a lot about how people lived during the Stone Age, and how they saw the world around them.

What does the proverb *a picture is worth a thousand words* mean?

Ⓐ A lot can be learned by studying a picture.

Ⓑ A lot can be learned from the pictures in a book.

Ⓒ No need to worry about something you cannot see.

Ⓓ Owning something is better than borrowing something.

6 The officials at Lascaux wanted to protect the paintings. What evidence from the text shows the solution to this problem?

Ⓕ Lascaux II was opened in 1983.

Ⓖ The caves were closed to the public.

Ⓗ Jacques Marsal became Chief Guardian.

Ⓘ The many visitors were damaging the paintings.

GO ON →

Name: ______________________ Date: __________

7 Read this sentence from the article.

The paintings of Lascaux are a window to the past.

What does this metaphor mean?

Ⓐ The paint is so thin that you can see through it.

Ⓑ The entrance to the cave leads you to the paintings.

Ⓒ These pictures help you see what the world was like long ago.

Ⓓ These images were painted on windows in the caves of Lascaux.

8 What information does the sidebar provide?

Ⓕ where Lascaux is located

Ⓖ how the painters made paint

Ⓗ where Jacques Marsal is today

Ⓘ what is shown in the cave paintings

9 Which word from the article is a homograph of the word defined below?

to carry on the body, as clothes

Ⓐ awe

Ⓑ ceiling

Ⓒ tunnel

Ⓓ wear

10 In order to help the reader understand the discovery at Lascaux, the author tells the story

Ⓕ in chronological order.

Ⓖ like a newspaper story.

Ⓗ with interviews.

Ⓘ in first person.

GO ON →

Name: ______________________________ Date: ________

Use "Keys to the Past" on pages 109 through 111 to answer Numbers 11 through 20.

11 Why was Jill feeling discouraged at the beginning of the passage?

Ⓐ She lost her trowel and gloves.

Ⓑ She did not know what the disc was.

Ⓒ She could not talk to Professor Quill.

Ⓓ She had not found any valuable artifacts.

12 Read this sentence from the passage.

Mounted on the top in the back was a black cylinder.

The Greek root of *cylinder* means "roll." Therefore, a *cylinder* is MOST likely

Ⓕ broken.

Ⓖ rounded.

Ⓗ stretched.

Ⓘ wrinkled.

13 Read this sentence from the passage.

Behind the rows was an array of thin metal rods arranged like a fan with tiny metal heads on the ends.

What does the similie *arranged like a fan* mean in this sentence?

Ⓐ spread out

Ⓑ wide at the top

Ⓒ quietly humming

Ⓓ poorly constructed

GO ON →

Name: ______________________ Date: ________

14 How does finding the bound papers help Jill figure out how the artifact was used? Support your answer with clear text evidence from the passage?

____

____

____

____

____

____

15 In the passage, Professor Quill is not available to check Jill's artifact. How does this help Jill?

Ⓐ she gets a chance to figure out what she is going to say

Ⓑ she stops digging thinks about the artifact she found

Ⓒ she keeps digging and finds the book and paper

Ⓓ she takes a break and gets some rest

16 Read this sentence from the passage.

"Doubt is the beginning, not the end, of wisdom."

What does this proverb MOST likely mean?

Ⓕ The wisest people believe nothing.

Ⓖ To gain wisdom, start at the beginning.

Ⓗ The wisest people never have any doubts.

Ⓘ Doubt makes you ask questions and helps you learn.

GO ON →

Name: ______________________________ Date: ________

17 What causes Professor Quill to tell Jill she has made an important discovery.

Ⓐ Jill digs up an artifact.

Ⓑ Professor Quill is out.

Ⓒ Jill returns to her digging.

Ⓓ Jill shows how the artifact works.

18 Use evidence from the text to show how you know the passage takes place in the future.

____

____

____

____

____

____

19 What is the MAIN problem in the passage?

Ⓐ The city is buried in dirt.

Ⓑ Nobody reads or writes any more.

Ⓒ The two archaeologists cannot agree.

Ⓓ The purpose of Jill's artifact is uncertain.

GO ON →

Name: ______________________________ Date: ________

Use "Lascaux: A Treasure in the Woods" and "The Buried City" to answer the question below.

20 Compare the discoveries in the article and the passage. Explain the similarities and differences using clear text evidence from the article and passage.

GO ON →

Read the passage "The Santa Fe Trail" before answering Numbers 21 through 30.

The Santa Fe Trail

In the 1800s, many trails crossed the American West. One of these was the Santa Fe Trail. Unlike most trails at the time, it was used mainly for trading. Other trails were used by settlers going to make a new life in the West.

For a while, Spain ruled the area around Santa Fe. The Spanish prohibited trade with the United States. After Mexico gained its freedom from Spain, trade between Mexico and the United States began. In 1821, William Becknell made a trip from Missouri to Santa Fe to trade. This was the first of many trips along the trail. The next year he came back with a wagon train full of goods. At its peak, the trail carried more than 2,000 wagons a year.

The trail was about 780 miles long. It took 40 to 60 days to reach Santa Fe from Missouri. It followed the Arkansas River, then it split. The first path went with the river to Bent's Fort in Colorado. It then turned south through a mountain pass to reach Santa Fe.

The Santa Fe Trail, 1850

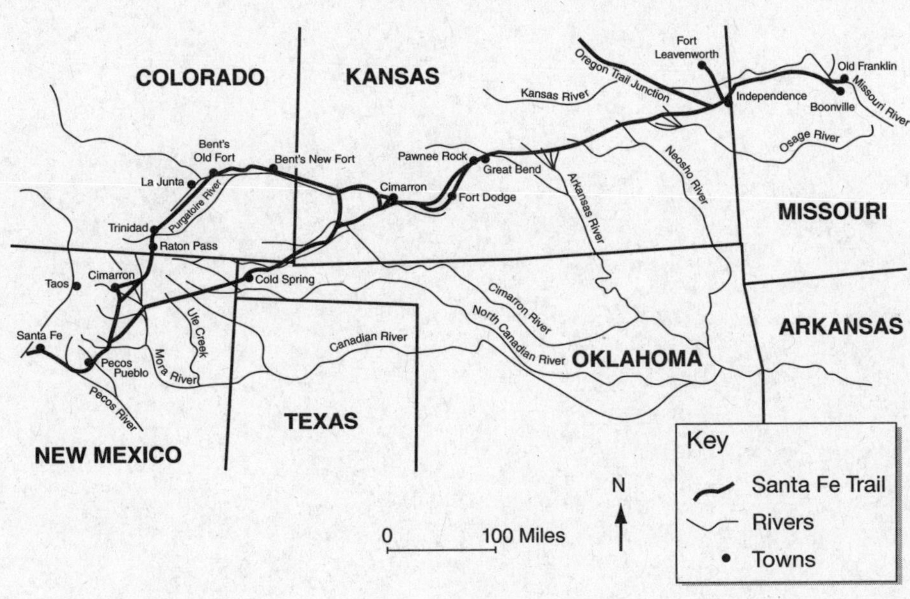

GO ON →

The second path went southwest to New Mexico and crossed the desert to Santa Fe. This path was shorter and easier for wagon trains to follow. It did not go through mountains like the first route. The desert was riskier, however. Travelers could run out of water in the desert.

The Pecos Pueblo

One of the last places the trail passed through was the Pecos Pueblo. This was a group of ruins. Some of the ruins were from an ancient settlement. Others were the remains of old Spanish missions. Stories about these ruins told of lost gold.

Like Santa Fe, the Pecos Pueblo was a trade center. The site was just right for trade. It linked the farming areas of the Rio Grande valley with the hunting areas of the plains. Around A.D. 800 many tribes came to trade, and they brought items such as buffalo hides, shells, pottery, and food.

Because of its value as a trading center, the Pecos Pueblo grew in size. Between the years 1450 to 1600, about 2,000 people lived at the site. They stayed in large buildings that were four or five stories high. They climbed ladders up to each floor, and these ladders could be pulled inside for safety.

GO ON →

The Arrival of the Spanish

In the early 1500s, Spanish explorers came upon the Pecos Pueblo. When the native people met the Spanish, they told stories about a place called Quivera. This was a city to the east that was supposed to be made of gold. More than likely, they told this story so the Spanish would go look for it and leave them alone. Their idea worked. The Spanish left to search for the lost city of gold. Of course, they never found it.

By the end of the 1500s, more Spanish had arrived. The Pecos Pueblo changed hands a number of times. While the Spanish were in control, they built a great church. This church did not survive for long, but another was built later. What is left of this church makes up the most impressive ruins at the site.

As the site kept changing hands, the people living there moved away. They were tired of the unrest. In 1838, the last people packed up and left. For most of the time the Santa Fe Trail was used, the Pecos Pueblo was a desert ruin.

The Santa Fe Trail was not used much after 1880. Once a railroad linked Santa Fe with other major trading cities, the trail was no longer needed.

Today, the trail attracts tourists instead of traders. Some people still study the trail to understand how it was used. A small group of people even travel the trail each year as a way to honor its history.

GO ON →

Name: ______________________________ Date: __________

21 The Santa Fe Trail was developed mainly for which group?

Ⓐ traders

Ⓑ missionaries

Ⓒ army soldiers

Ⓓ settlers moving west

22 The Pecos Pueblo developed as a trading center overtime. What evidence in the text supports the idea that this took a long time?

____

____

____

____

____

____

23 Read these sentences from the article.

The first path went with the river to Bent's Fort in Colorado. It then turned south through a mountain pass to reach Santa Fe.

Which meaning fits *pass* as it is used in the sentence above?

Ⓐ narrow route or road

Ⓑ throw a ball, as in football

Ⓒ permission to come and go

Ⓓ move past or around something

GO ON →

Name: ______________________________ Date: ________

24 Which of these events happened FIRST in the history of the Pecos Pueblo?

Ⓕ Pecos Pueblo became a trading center.

Ⓖ William Becknell traveled to Santa Fe.

Ⓗ Spanish missionaries came to Pecos.

Ⓘ Spaniards began looking for Quivera.

25 Read this sentence from the article.

The desert was riskier, however. Travelers could run out of water in the desert.

Which word has the OPPOSITE meaning of *riskier* as used in the sentence above?

Ⓐ better

Ⓑ easier

Ⓒ safer

Ⓓ wider

26 The author describes how life changed at the Pecos Pueblo. What evidence from the text shows the event that caused the most change?

Ⓕ All of the people left Pecos Pueblo.

Ⓖ A church was built at the Pecos Pueblo.

Ⓗ Spanish explorers came to Pecos Pueblo.

Ⓘ Many tribes went to the Pecos Pueblo to trade.

GO ON →

Name: ______________________________ Date: ________

27 The author explains that the people of Pecos Pueblo told the Spanish about the city called Quivera to show that

Ⓐ they wanted the Spanish to go away.

Ⓑ they needed the Spanish to destroy it.

Ⓒ they hoped the Spanish would build a mission there.

Ⓓ they knew the Spanish would not survive a trip there.

28 If you visited Pecos Pueblo in 1600, what would you have seen there?

Ⓕ a railroad station

Ⓖ four-story buildings

Ⓗ the ruins of a pueblo

Ⓘ American wagon trains

29 Read these sentences from the article.

> **The Spanish prohibited trade with the United States. After Mexico gained its freedom from Spain, trade between Mexico and the United States began.**

Which word has the OPPOSITE meaning of *prohibited* as used in the sentence above?

Ⓐ allowed

Ⓑ ignored

Ⓒ outlawed

Ⓓ taxed

GO ON →

Name: ______________________ Date: __________

30 Explain why the author describes the challenges travelers faced on the northern and southern paths of the Santa Fe Trail. Support your explanation with clear text evidence from the article.

GO ON →

The passage below is a first draft written by Markeisha. It contains mistakes. Read the passage to answer questions 31 through 40.

(1) My grandmother has the most knowledge about this town than anyone. (2) She's the thoughtfulest person I know. (3) She has also lived here all her life. (4) However, them facts can't explain how she knows so much. (5) My gray-haired old good granddad has lived here all his life, too. (6) But his knowledge of history is worser than mine.

(7) "I just keep my eyes and ears open," Grandma says.

(8) "Don't we all do that?" I ask.

(9) "Most folks just see and hear," she explains, "but I try to look and listen."

(10) Surely that can't be her secret—or is it?

(11) "It is," she says. (12) "You want to know the true history of a small american town? (13) Talk to the people who live there. (14) They're smartest than you think. (15) The old folks can tell you things going back 60 or 70 years before you were born. (16) I'm good at letting folks talk. (17) I got to know our town. (18) This town is an very interesting place."

(19) I enjoy listening to my grandma talk. (20) I enjoy it more than anything.

GO ON →

Name: ______________________ Date: ________

31 How can sentence 1 best be written?

Ⓐ My grandmother has morer knowledge about this town than anyone.

Ⓑ My grandmother has the more knowledge about this town than anyone.

Ⓒ My grandmother has moster knowledge about this town than anyone.

Ⓓ My grandmother has more knowledge about this town than anyone.

32 How can sentence 2 best be written?

Ⓕ She's the most thoughtfulest person I know.

Ⓖ She's the thoughtfuler person I know.

Ⓗ She's the most thoughtful person I know.

Ⓘ She's the more thoughtfuler person I know.

33 Which is the correct way to write sentence 4?

Ⓐ However, the facts can't explain how she knows so much.

Ⓑ However, those facts can't explain how she knows so much.

Ⓒ However, a facts can't explain how she knows so much.

Ⓓ However, this facts can't explain how she knows so much.

GO ON →

Name: ______________________ Date: ________

34 How can sentence 5 best be written?

Ⓕ My good, grey-haired, old granddad has lived here all his life, too.

Ⓖ My gray-haired good old granddad has lived here all his life, too.

Ⓗ My old good grey-haired granddad has lived here all his life, too.

Ⓘ My good old gray-haired granddad has lived here all his life, too.

35 How can sentence 6 be written correctly?

Ⓐ But his knowledge of history is badder than mine.

Ⓑ But his knowledge of history is more bad than mine.

Ⓒ But his knowledge of history is worse than mine.

Ⓓ But his knowledge of history is worst than mine.

36 How can sentence 12 be written correctly?

Ⓕ You want to know the true history of a Small american town?

Ⓖ You want to know the true history of a small American Town?

Ⓗ You want to know the true history of a Small American town?

Ⓘ You want to know the true history of a small American town?

GO ON →

Name: ______________________________ Date: ________

37 How can sentence 14 best be written?

Ⓐ They're smarter than you think.

Ⓑ They're more smarter than you think.

Ⓒ They're most smarter than you think.

Ⓓ They're more smart than you think.

38 How can sentences 16 and 17 best be combined?

Ⓕ I'm good at letting folks talk, but I got to know our town.

Ⓖ Because I'm good at letting folks talk, I got to know our town.

Ⓗ I'm good at letting folks talk because I got to know our town.

Ⓘ Letting folks talk, I'm good at getting to know our town.

39 How can sentence 18 best be written?

Ⓐ This town is a very interesting place.

Ⓑ This town is the very interesting place.

Ⓒ This town is this very interesting place.

Ⓓ This town is that very interesting place.

40 How can sentences 19 and 20 best be combined?

Ⓕ I enjoy listening more than anything, and my grandma talks.

Ⓖ More than anything, my grandma enjoys listening and talking.

Ⓗ I enjoy listening to my grandma talk more than anything.

Ⓘ More than listening, I enjoy my grandma talking about anything.

STOP

Writing Prompt – Narrative

Imagine you are walking down a particular street in your city or town. How do your senses help you understand the world around you? Write an essay telling what you see, hear, smell, feel, and taste when walking down this street. Use the space below to plan your writing then write your essay on a separate sheet of paper.

Answer Key

Name: ______________________

Question	Answer	Content Focus	CCSS	Complexity
1	C	Text Structure: Sequence	RI.4.5	DOK 1
2	H	Greek Roots	L.4.4b	DOK 1
3	See below	Text Structure: Sequence	RI.4.3	DOK 2
4	G	Text Structure: Problem and Solution	RI.4.5	DOK 2
5	A	Figurative Language: Proverbs and Adages	L.4.5b	DOK 2
6	G	Text Structure: Problem and Solution	RI.4.5	DOK 2
7	C	Figurative Language: Similes and Metaphors	L.4.5a	DOK 2
8	I	Text Features: Sidebar	RI.4.7	DOK 1
9	D	Homographs	L.4.4	DOK 1
10	F	Text Structure: Sequence	RI.4.5	DOK 2
11	D	Character, Setting, Plot: Cause and Effect	RL.4.3	DOK 1
12	G	Greek Roots	L.4.4b	DOK 1
13	A	Figurative Language: Similes and Metaphors	L.4.5a	DOK 2
14	See below	Character, Setting, Plot: Problem and Solution	RL.4.3	DOK 2
15	C	Character, Setting, Plot: Cause and Effect	RL.4.3	DOK 2
16	I	Character, Setting, Plot: Cause and Effect	RL.4.3	DOK 2
17	D	Figurative Language: Proverbs and Adages	L.4.5b	DOK 2
18	See below	Character, Setting, Plot: Problem and Solution	RL.4.3	DOK 2
19	D	Character, Setting, Plot: Problem and Solution	RL.4.3	DOK 2
20	See below	Compare Across Texts	RL.4.3	DOK 4
21	A	Main Idea and Key Details	RI.4.2	DOK 1
22	See below	Text Structure: Sequence	RI.4.3	DOK 2

Answer Key Name: ______________________

Question	Answer	Content Focus	CCSS	Complexity
23	A	Homographs	L.4.4a	DOK 1
24	I	Sequence	RI.4.5	DOK 1
25	C	Context Clues: Antonyms	L.4.5c	DOK 2
26	H	Sequence	RI.4.5	DOK 1
27	A	Text Structure: Problem and Solution	RI.4.5	DOK 2
28	G	Main Idea and Key Details	RI.4.2	DOK 1
29	A	Context Clues: Antonyms	L.4.5c	DOK 2
30	See below	Text Structure: Problem and Solution	RI.4.5	DOK 3
31	D	Adjectives That Compare	L.3.1g	DOK 1
32	H	Adjectives	L.3.1g	DOK 1
33	B	Articles	L.3.1a	DOK 1
34	I	Ordering Adjectives	L.4.1d	DOK 1
35	C	Combining Sentences	L.4.1f	DOK 1
36	I	Capitalize Proper Adjectives	L.4.2a	DOK 1
37	A	Adjectives That Compare	L.3.1g	DOK 1
38	G	Comparing with Good and Bad	L.4.2c	DOK 2
39	A	Articles	L.3.1g	DOK 1
40	H	Comparing with More and Most	L.4.2c	DOK 2
Writing Prompt	See below	Narrative	W.4.3a–e	DOK 3

Comprehension: Multiple-Choice 1, 4, 6, 8, 10–11, 15–16, 19–21, 24, 26–28	/14	%
Comprehension: Constructed Response 3, 14, 18, 20, 22, 30	/16	%
Vocabulary 3, 5, 7, 9, 12–13, 17, 25, 26, 29	/10	%
Grammar, Mechanics, Usage 31–40	/10	%
Total Unit Assessment Score	/50	%

Answer Key Name: ______________________________

3 Response should note that the boys walked into the woods; they heard their dog barking and went to investigate; they fell into a cave. One boy lit a lamp, and they found the paintings.

14 Students should note that the bound pages of *Treasure Island* and the pile of sheets are paper. The pages of *Treasure Island* are covered in symbols like the ones on the buttons and the rods. They should also note that the buttons, rod, and cylinder are parts of a typewriter. Jill discovers that putting a sheet of paper into the typewriter and striking the keys creates symbols on the paper which are similar to those in the book.

18 Students should note that this story takes place in the distant future. The title suggests they are trying to solve a mystery related to something from the past. Jill finds a typewriter and a book, but no one knows what they are. They are found at an archaeological site, and Professor Quill says they are at least 4,000 years old.

20 Students should note that both discoveries are made by young people, and both involve ancient artifacts. The four teenagers find cave paintings by accident; Jill finds a typewriter and a book while digging at an archaeological site. Both discoveries reveal information about cultures of long ago, how they lived, and what their worlds were like. The cave paintings come from the distant past and a culture that seems primitive to us. The typewriter comes from our present, but our culture seems primitive to people of the future.

22 Its position was ideal for trade between farmers of the Rio Grande valley and hunter tribes of the plains. Trade flourished during the 16th century, with increasing numbers of people both passing through and settling. The trail became busy when Mexico freed itself from Spanish rule and the embargo on U.S.-Mexico trade was lifted.

30 Students should describe the two paths and compare their advantages and disadvantages. Both started in Missouri and went across Kansas. The northern path followed the Arkansas River into Colorado and went to a fort, which could provide protection and supplies. Then it went through a mountain pass, which could be difficult for wagons. The southern route did not follow a river and did not go through mountains. It passed through a small part of Oklahoma and into New Mexico. It was much easier for wagon travel, but it did not go past any forts and it did go through a desert, which could be risky if travelers ran out of water.

Writing Prompt

Refer to the scoring criteria in the Teacher Introduction.

Read the next two articles. Then answer the questions that follow.

A History of the Bicycle

The bicycles we ride today are light, safe, fast, and fun. However, this has not always been so. The first bicycles were built in Europe and the United States in the early 1800s. They were heavy, slow, and dangerous. These early bicycles were called Hobbyhorses. They had heavy wooden frames and two wooden wheels. Riders had to push them forward with their feet. Using one was more like running than riding. In fact, the German word for these early bicycles means "running machines."

Soon, some people improved the Hobbyhorse by finding ways to move it more easily. In Scotland, in about 1839, Kirkpatrick MacMillan added foot pedals that were connected to the rear wheel by long rods. About 50 years later a Frenchman named Pierre Michaux, and his son Ernst, improved these foot pedals and added a crank to the front wheel. Their bicycle made cycling popular. Some historians question if Pierre and Ernst worked alone, but they are generally recognized as creating what we think of as the modern bicycle.

Even so, the bicycle needed a lot more work before it could really serve as a good means of transportation. The Michaux bicycle had a front wheel that was much larger than the rear wheel. It was faster than the Hobbyhorse, but it toppled over very easily. The Michaux bicycle was as uncomfortable as the Hobbyhorse, too. It also ground along the roads making a loud noise.

The heavy, wooden wheels rimmed with iron made for a very rough ride. For this reason, the Michaux bicycle became known as the Boneshaker.

GO ON →

In the early 1870s, a high-wheeled bicycle was developed in England. It was called the Penny Farthing. Like the Michaux bicycle, it had one very large front wheel, and two small back wheels. On some bicycles, the front wheel was five feet high. These high-wheeled bicycles could go quite fast, but they were hard to handle. They often threw their riders!

Later inventors made more improvements to the bicycle. In the 1880s, bicycle makers stopped making the front wheels so large. The bicycle as we know it came into being soon after. Still, designers kept working to make bicycles safer, faster, and easier to use.

It is lucky for us that people continued to improve the bicycle. Today's safe, comfortable bicycles are enjoyed all over the world. These wonderful machines are widely used for transportation and for exercise. Inventors of the bicycle should take a bow.

The First Bike?

Leonardo da Vinci (1452–1519) was a famous painter. He was also an inventive genius. Leonardo studied how things worked in nature. He filled notebooks with detailed drawings. Then he used these studies to dream up new machines. His designs included a helicopter, a robot, and many other ideas. But did he also invent the first bicycle?

Experts were very surprised when a bicycle sketch drawn by Leonardo was published in a 1974 book. The editor said the drawing was found in one of Leonardo's notebooks on the back of another drawing. The discovery caused a lot of argument. Many experts did not think the sketch looked like Leonardo's work. Some suggested it was made by one of his students. Then a scholar who had examined the same notebook in 1961 spoke up. He said the drawing had not been there at the time he studied the notebook.

Today, most experts believe the bicycle drawing is a fake. We still are not sure who made it or when.

GO ON →

Biking to the Top

Greg LeMond did not always dream of being a bicyclist. As a kid, he loved skiing. Greg only began cycling to keep in shape. Once he started, though, he quickly became a star. In his very first race, at age 15, he came in second place even though his bike was not meant for racing.

In 1978, 17-year-old Greg made a list of cycling goals. All of them began with the word "Win." Within a few years, he had achieved all but one.

Early Successes

Greg's first goal was to win the 1979 Junior World Championship in Argentina. This road race covered about 72 miles. Greg had already been in another, shorter race and was a little tired. Still, he rode well until another rider tried to run him off the road. That racer was thrown out of the race, making Greg the winner. He was the first American to win this race.

The next goal was the 1980 Olympics in Moscow. Greg was on the American cycling team. However, after the Soviet army invaded another country, the United States protested by keeping its Olympic teams home. Greg missed that chance to race against many of the world's best riders.

In 1980, Greg became a professional racer. He moved to Europe and entered a lot of races. In Switzerland in 1983, he met his third goal by winning the World Cycling Championship. The fact that he was the first American to win was icing on the cake. Now Greg turned to his final goal: the Tour de France.

GO ON →

Tour de France

The Tour de France is the most famous bicycle race in the world. It lasts three weeks and covers more than 1,920 miles. About 200 men participate. Each day, the racers cover a certain distance. Their times for each day are added up. At the end, the one with the shortest total time is the winner. Sometimes cyclists are on a team with other riders. They often work together to help the strongest team member win the race.

The Tour route varies but is always demanding. Climbing steep mountain roads is very hard. Speeding back down is very dangerous. Other cyclists and watchers often get in the way. Many who start the race do not finish.

In Greg's first Tour in 1984, he took third place; the next year, he came in second. Many claim that Greg could have won in 1985 if the coach had not made him hold back to help a teammate win.

Finally, Greg's turn came. In 1986, he slowly worked his way into the lead. Each day, the person with the shortest time to that point wears a special yellow shirt. Greg earned the shirt on the seventeenth day and kept it until the end. When he crossed the finish line in Paris, Greg became the first non-European rider to ever win the Tour de France.

GO ON →

Overcoming Disaster

In 1987, Greg faced a huge challenge when he almost died after a hunting accident. Few people expected him to ever race again, but Greg proved them wrong—he started training again only eight weeks after the accident. He also set a new goal for himself: winning the Tour de France again.

In 1989, Greg was back in the yellow shirt, riding even faster than in 1986. He won that Tour and, amazingly, also won the World Cycling Championship two months later. He earned his third (and last) Tour de France victory in 1990. Though illness forced Greg to quit racing in 1994, he stayed connected to the sport through his business and other activities.

Greg's 1978 list of goals did not include "Be remembered as one of the greatest cyclists of all times." But if it had, that would be one more goal achieved.

LeMond's Speeds Compared with Other Tour de France Winners, 1903–2011

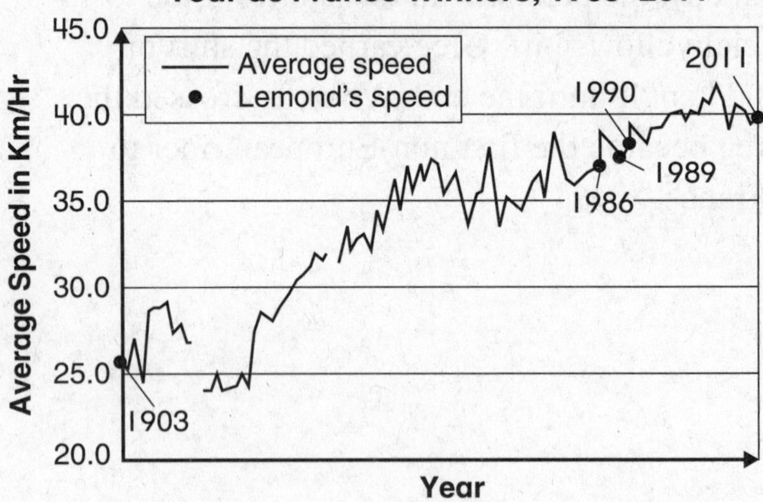

(Note: 30 kilometers per hour equals about 19 miles per hour; the breaks in data show the years the race did not take place due to World Wars I and II.)

GO ON →

Name: ______________________ Date: ________

Use "A History of the Bicycle" on pages 134–135 to answer Numbers 1 through 10.

1 What is the MAIN idea of this article?

Ⓐ The first bicycles built in the early 1800s had some problems, but bicycles have been greatly improved since then.

Ⓑ Early bicycles were built in Europe and the United States, but using them was more like running than riding.

Ⓒ Today's bicycles are safe and comfortable, and they are widely used for transportation and for exercise.

Ⓓ The bicycles built in the early 1800s needed a lot of work to make them useful for transportation.

2 Inventors continued to make improvements to the bicycle through the 1800s. Which key detail BEST supports this idea?

Ⓕ Penny Farthing bicycles often threw their riders.

Ⓖ The first bicycles were heavy, slow, and dangerous.

Ⓗ Bicycles are widely used for transportation and for exercise.

Ⓘ Kirkpatrick MacMillan connected foot pedals to the rear wheels.

3 According to the text, how did people move the Hobbyhorse bicycle?

Ⓐ by turning a crank

Ⓑ by coasting downhill

Ⓒ by pushing with their feet

Ⓓ by pedaling with their legs

GO ON →

Name: ______________________________ Date: __________

4 Which of these improvements was necessary before bicycles became easier to handle?

Ⓕ making a very large front wheel with two small back wheels

Ⓖ adding iron rims to heavy wooden wheels

Ⓗ connecting pedals to the rear wheel

Ⓘ making the front wheel smaller

5 Why was the sidebar included with this article?

Ⓐ to describe some Leonardo da Vinci inventions

Ⓑ to explain how the earliest bicycle came into being

Ⓒ to add new information about the history of bicycles

Ⓓ to prove that Leonardo da Vinci designed the first bicycle

6 Read this sentence from the article.

The discovery caused a lot of argument.

The use of *argument* instead of *discussion* suggests that many experts

Ⓕ were unsure about the truth.

Ⓖ did not believe the editor.

Ⓗ had very strong opinions.

Ⓘ agreed with each other.

GO ON →

Name: ______________________________ Date: ________

7 What is the MAIN idea of the last paragraph on page 135?

Ⓐ People all over the world still use bicycles.

Ⓑ Inventors have tried to make bicycles safer.

Ⓒ Today's bicycles are both useful and enjoyable.

Ⓓ Bicycles are machines that serve many purposes.

8 Read this sentence from the article.

Inventors of the bicycle should take a bow.

Which definition fits *bow* as it is used in the sentence above?

Ⓕ a knot with two or more loops extending from it

Ⓖ a forward bending of the upper body

Ⓗ to bend under a weight

Ⓘ a branch of a tree

9 Which word from the article has a positive connotation?

Ⓐ heavy

Ⓑ popular

Ⓒ toppled

Ⓓ transportation

10 What text evidence shows why many experts believe the Leonardo bike sketch is a fake?

Ⓕ Leonardo da Vinci (1452–1519) was a famous painter.

Ⓖ Then he used these studies to dream up new machines.

Ⓗ His designs included a helicopter, a robot, and many other ideas.

Ⓘ Many experts did not think the sketch looked like Leonardo's work.

GO ON →

Name: ______________________________ Date: __________

Use "Biking to the Top" on pages 136–138 to answer Numbers 11 through 20.

11 What is the MAIN idea of the article?

Ⓐ Though he could have been a great skier, Greg LeMond chose cycling instead.

Ⓑ When he was very young, Greg LeMond set some high goals for himself.

Ⓒ Winning the Tour de France was Greg LeMond's biggest challenge.

Ⓓ Greg LeMond was one of the greatest cyclists of all time.

12 Why did the author include the graph with this article?

____

____

____

____

____

13 Based on the graph, which statement is true?

Ⓐ In general, winning speeds have increased since the race started in 1903.

Ⓑ Each year's winner went faster than the winner of the year before.

Ⓒ The 2003 winner went about twice as fast as the 1903 winner.

Ⓓ The highest winning speeds occurred in the 1980s.

GO ON →

Name: ______________________________ Date: __________

14 Explain what prevented Greg from competing in the 1980 Olympics? Support your answer with clear text evidence from the article.

____

____

____

____

____

____

15 Read this sentence from the article.

The fact that he was the first American to win was icing on the cake.

What does this sentence mean?

Ⓐ Being the first American winner made the experience even more special.

Ⓑ After becoming the first American winner, he got a special dessert.

Ⓒ The first American winner got to cut the winner's cake.

Ⓓ A special prize was given to the first American winner.

16 What is the MOST important idea in the Early Successes section of the article?

Ⓕ Greg's first goal was to win the Junior World Championship.

Ⓖ Greg LeMond achieved his goals one by one.

Ⓗ In 1980, Greg became a professional racer.

Ⓘ He was the first American world champion.

GO ON →

Name: ______________________________ Date: ________

17 Read this sentence from the article.

Many claim that Greg could have won in 1985 if the coach had not made him hold back to help a teammate win.

Which word has a connotation MOST similar to that of *claim*?

Ⓐ believe

Ⓑ doubt

Ⓒ reply

Ⓓ understand

18 Read this sentence from the article.

When he crossed the finish line in Paris, Greg became the first non-European rider to ever win the Tour de France.

What does *non-European* mean?

Ⓕ one who is European

Ⓖ against Europeans

Ⓗ before Europeans

Ⓘ not European

19 Which key detail BEST supports the idea that Greg was a good cyclist?

Ⓐ Another racer tried to run him off the road during this event.

Ⓑ He finished third the first time he entered the Tour.

Ⓒ He held the lead from Day 17 until the end.

Ⓓ His coach asked him to help a teammate.

GO ON →

Name: ______________________________ Date: ________

Use "A History of the Bicycle" and "Biking to the Top" to answer the question below.

20 How do these articles show the effects of a continued desire to improve? Support your response with clear text evience from the articles.

GO ON →

Read the passage "A Big New World" before answering Numbers 21 through 30.

A Big New World

As the train finally gasped to a halt, Hattie grabbed her bag. She was eager to start her first visit to the city. She climbed down to the platform and quickly found her waiting relatives. Uncle Harold's car was a brand-new 1915 Ford Model T. As the group headed toward it, Hattie admired Cousin Lillian's fancy clothes. But she noticed they seemed to make walking rather hard.

Riding in the automobile was quite an experience. Cars elbowed past like people at a crowded party. Horns blasted constantly. Stinky fumes from all those engines made Hattie feel ill. When Hattie remarked on all this, Lillian was puzzled. "This is not very much traffic," she said. "Are there many cars where you live?" She couldn't believe it when Hattie said no and that the few cars they had didn't all go out on the road at once.

After a slow trip across town, they arrived at a tall brick house with a red front door. Inside, Aunt Mabel exclaimed, "Better late than never!" Then she briskly steered Hattie into the warm front room. Hattie was very happy to accept the welcoming arms of a big, soft armchair. She tried answering her aunt's questions but could not help yawning. Aunt Mabel suggested an early bedtime.

Hattie was amazed by the washroom upstairs. At home, they took baths in a tub they carried into the kitchen. They heated water from the well on the woodstove. This was a long process, so they did not take baths often. Here, you had both hot and cold water, coming right into the house. You didn't have to preheat the water or carry anything!

During the night, Hattie woke to the sound of something clanking and hissing in her room. She cried out, frightened, and her uncle quickly appeared.

GO ON →

"It's only steam in the radiator," he said, pointing to a large metal object along the wall. "It's noisy. All these new houses heat with steam instead of fireplaces." Hattie heard Lillian across the hall asking, "Hasn't she ever seen a radiator before?"

In the morning, Hattie stood in the kitchen doorway. The maid, Nora, was cooking breakfast. The kitchen was very new and modern-looking. The sink had hot and cold faucets just like the washroom. The white monster squatting in the corner turned out to be a refrigerator. The stove had metal coils that heated up when you turned some handles. Nora said it ran on electricity, not wood. Hattie had heard about these inventions but had never seen them.

"Would you like some toast?" asked Nora. Mmmmmm! Hattie nodded. Nora attached the bread to a metal box with wire racks on the outside. She plugged this into the wall, and it started to glow.

"When one side gets brown, turn this knob to toast the other side," she said. "Watch carefully so it doesn't burn."

Hattie knew about watching toast. At home they made toast over the fire on a toasting fork. How was this machine an improvement?

Hattie soon discovered that her relatives owned *all* of the latest gadgets. They also took pride in showing off their up-to-date city. Lillian was amused when Hattie exclaimed about the modern marvels on every corner. To Lillian, all these things were ordinary. She didn't understand that Hattie was seeing a new world—strange, exciting, and a little bit scary.

When Hattie returned home, she told her parents about all she had seen. "Some of those new things do make life easier. But sometimes they're not any easier, or they cause problems."

Hattie's father replied, "The challenge is figuring out when a new way of doing something is really better. Now, how about some old-fashioned toast?"

GO ON →

Name: ______________________________ Date: ________

Now answer Numbers 21 through 30. Base your answers on "A Big New World."

21 What text evidence BEST tells the author's message?

Ⓐ "Some of those new things do make life easier."

Ⓑ Hattie had heard about these inventions but had never seen them.

Ⓒ Hattie soon discovered that her relatives owned *all* of the latest gadgets.

Ⓓ "The challenge is figuring out when a new way of doing something is really better."

22 Read this sentence from the passage.

As the train finally gasped to a halt, Hattie grabbed her bag.

How does the personification of the train as it "gasped to a halt" help the reader understand what the train is doing?

Ⓕ People had trouble breathing while the train was moving.

Ⓖ The train moved like a person who is exercising hard.

Ⓗ Something was wrong with the train's engine.

Ⓘ The train made steam noises as it stopped.

GO ON →

Name: ______________________________ Date: ________

23 Read this sentence from the passage.

Hattie was very happy to accept the welcoming arms of a big, soft armchair.

What mood does the author create by using the phrase "the welcoming arms of a big, soft armchair" in this sentence? Support your answer with clear text evidence from the passage.

____

____

____

____

____

____

24 Read these sentences from the passage.

Inside, Aunt Mabel exclaimed, "Better late than never!" Then she briskly steered Hattie into the warm front room.

What does the saying *better late than never* mean?

Ⓕ It's better for something good to happen later than you expect than not to happen at all.

Ⓖ It's better not to get impatient when you're waiting for something to happen.

Ⓗ When you're waiting for someone to arrive, time seems to move very slowly.

Ⓘ Everything in life seems to take longer than people expect or plan for.

GO ON →

Name: ______________________________ Date: __________

25 Use text evidence to explain how the author uses Lillian to show the differences in the way people live their lives.

____

____

____

____

____

____

26 Which of the following details adds to the imagery of the passage?

Ⓕ Watch carefully so it doesn't burn.

Ⓖ Cars elbowed past like people at a crowded party.

Ⓗ You didn't have to preheat the water or carry anything!

Ⓘ They also took pride in showing off their up-to-date city.

GO ON →

Name: ________________________________ Date: ________

27 Which words from the passage are homophones?

Ⓐ maid/made

Ⓑ not/nodded

Ⓒ soon/sound

Ⓓ wire/were

28 Read this sentence from the passage.

The white monster squatting in the corner turned out to be a refrigerator.

The author compares the refrigerator to a monster to show that

Ⓕ Hattie was afraid of both monsters and refrigerators.

Ⓖ a monster changed itself to look like a refrigerator.

Ⓗ the refrigerator was large and strange-looking.

Ⓘ Hattie thought the refrigerator was ugly.

29 Read this sentence from the passage.

You didn't have to preheat the water or carry anything!

What does *preheat* mean?

Ⓐ not heat

Ⓑ heat after

Ⓒ heat again

Ⓓ heat before

GO ON →

Name: ______________________ Date: ________

30 How does the first paragraph on page 146 of set up the rest of the story? Support your answer with clear text evidence from the passage.

GO ON →

The passage below is a first draft written by Farah. It contains mistakes. Read the passage to answer Numbers 31 through 35.

(1) Grandma moved to the United States many years ago. (2) She learned right away that foods were different here. (3) She couldn't hardly find some of the ingredients she needed for her recipes. (4) She had to do her best with whatever she could buy in the market. (5) For example, one of her favorite dishes is a spicy soup called *tongseng*. (6) On Java the island where she grew up, this is usually made, with goat meat. (7) You can't buy goat meat in most American stores. (8) Grandma started making *tongseng* with lamb or beef instead. (9) Her *tongseng* tastes the more yummy of all the soups in the world. (10) I'm happy that it is part of my family background.

GO ON →

Name: ______________________________ Date: ________

31 The prepositional phrase in sentence 1 tells

Ⓐ where Grandma moved.

Ⓑ what Grandma learned.

Ⓒ when Grandma moved.

Ⓓ how Grandma learned.

32 How can sentence 3 best be written?

Ⓕ She could not hardly find some of the ingredients she needed for her recipes.

Ⓖ She couldn't not find some of the ingredients she needed for her recipes.

Ⓗ She couldn't find some of the ingredients she needed for her recipes.

Ⓘ She couldn't find none of the ingredients she needed for her recipes.

33 Which is a prepositional phrase in sentence 4?

Ⓐ had to

Ⓑ do her best

Ⓒ whatever she could buy

Ⓓ in the market

GO ON →

Name: ______________________________ Date: ________

34 How can sentence 6 best be written?

Ⓕ On Java the island where she grew up this is usually made with goat meat.

Ⓖ On Java, the island where she grew up this is usually made with goat meat.

Ⓗ On Java the island, where she grew up this is usually made with goat meat.

Ⓘ On Java, the island where she grew up, this is usually made with goat meat.

35 How can sentence 9 best be written?

Ⓐ Her *tongseng* tastes the yummier of all the soups in the world.

Ⓑ Her *tongseng* tastes the yummiest of all the soups in the world.

Ⓒ Her *tongseng* tastes the more yummier of all the soups in the world.

Ⓓ Her *tongseng* tastes the most yummiest of all the soups in the world.

GO ON →

Read the article below. Choose the answer that correctly completes Numbers 36 through 40.

One day in 1941, Georges de Mestral was out hiking in the Swiss woods. Stopping to rest, he found a lot of burrs sticking firmly __(36)__ his clothes. His dog's shaggy coat was covered with the pesky seed pods, too, and they __(37)__ come off easily. De Mestral studied the burrs __(38)__. Their surfaces were covered with a lot of tiny hooks. This gave de Mestral an idea. The burrs could provide a new way to fasten clothing. People needed something that worked __(39)__ than zippers. Zippers often broke or got stuck.

De Mestral started trying out different ideas. He finally came up with a strip of tiny nylon loops that would grab __(40)__ onto a strip of tiny nylon hooks. In 1955, de Mestral registered his invention under the name Velcro.

GO ON →

Name: ________________________________ Date: ________

36 Which answer should go in blank (36)?

Ⓕ beside

Ⓖ for

Ⓗ to

37 Which answer should go in blank (37)?

Ⓐ didn't not

Ⓑ didn't hardly

Ⓒ did not

38 Which answer should go in blank (38)?

Ⓕ careful

Ⓖ carefully

Ⓗ more careful

39 Which answer should go in blank (39)?

Ⓐ better

Ⓑ more better

Ⓒ more good

40 Which answer should go in blank (40)?

Ⓕ tight

Ⓖ tightly

Ⓗ tightest

STOP

Writing Prompt – Persuassive

Choose a toy, game, or gadget that you know a lot about. Write a magazine article in which you give your opinion about the toy, game, or gadget. Support your opinion with details and reasons. Use the space below to plan your writing. Write your article on a separate sheet of paper.

Answer Key

Name: ____________________

Question	Answer	Content Focus	CCSS	Complexity
1	A	Main Idea and Key Details	RI.4.2	DOK 2
2	I	Main Idea and Key Details	RI.4.2	DOK 1
3	C	Main Idea and Key Details	RI.4.2	DOK 1
4	I	Main Idea and Key Details	RI.4.2	DOK 1
5	C	Text Features: Sidebars	RI.4.7	DOK 2
6	H	Connotation and Denotation	L.4.5	DOK 2
7	C	Main Idea and Key Details	RI.4.2	DOK 2
8	G	Homophones	L.4.4a	DOK 1
9	B	Connotation and Denotation	L.4.5	DOK 2
10	I	Text Features: Sidebars	RI.4.7	DOK 3
11	D	Main Idea and Key Details	RI.4.2	DOK 2
12	See below	Text Features: Graph	RI.4.7	DOK 2
13	A	Text Features: Graph	RI.4.7	DOK 2
14	See below	Main Idea and Key Details	RI.4.2	DOK 2
15	A	Figurative Language: Metaphors	L.4.5a	DOK 2
16	G	Latin and Greek Prefixes	L.4.4b	DOK 1
17	A	Connotation and Denotation	L.4.5	DOK 1
18	I	Main Idea and Key Details	RI.4.2	DOK 1
19	C	Main Idea and Key Details	RI.4.2	DOK 1
20	See below	Compare Across Texts	RI.4.9	DOK 4
21	D	Theme	RL.4.2	DOK 3
22	I	Literary Elements: Personification	RL.4.5	DOK 2

Answer Key Name: ______________________________

Question	Answer	Content Focus	CCSS	Complexity
23	See below	Literary Elements: Imagery; Personification	RL.4.5	DOK 2
24	F	Figurative Language: Proverbs and Adages	L.4.5b	DOK 2
25	See below	Theme	RL.4.2	DOK 3
26	G	Literary Elements: Imagery	RL.4.5	DOK 2
27	A	Homophones	L.4.4	DOK 1
28	H	Metaphors	L.4.5a	DOK 2
29	D	Latin and Greek Prefixes	L.4.4b	DOK 1
30	See below	Theme	RL.4.2	DOK 3
31	A	Sentences Using Prepositions	L.4.1e	DOK 1
32	H	Negatives	L.4.1	DOK 1
33	D	Prepositions	L.4.1e	DOK 1
34	I	Sentences Using Prepositions	L.4.1e	DOK 1
35	B	Comparing with Adverbs	L.4.2	DOK 1
36	H	Prepositions	L.4.1e	DOK 1
37	C	Negatives	L.4.1	DOK 1
38	G	Adverbs	L.4.1a	DOK 1
39	A	Comparing with Adverbs	L.4.2	DOK 1
40	G	Adverbs	L.4.1a	DOK 1
Writing Prompt	See below	Persuasive Writing	W.4.1a-d	DOK 3

Comprehension: Multiple-Choice 1–5, 7, 11, 13, 18–19, 21–22, 25–26	/14	%
Comprehension: Constructed Response 10, 12, 14, 20, 23, 25, 30	/16	%
Vocabulary 6, 8–9, 15–17, 24, 27, 29	/9	%
Grammar, Mechanics, Usage 31–40	/10	%
Total Unit Assessment Score	/50	%

12 The purpose of the graph is to compare LeMond's speeds in the Tour de France with those of other winners.

14 Greg was a member of the 1980 Olympic team but did not compete at the Olympics in Moscow. The United States protested the Soviet invasion of another country by keeping its Olympic team out of the Olympics that year.

20 Responses should be in paragraph form. Both of these articles describe striving to improve, to continue getting better. In "A History of the Bicycle," the article describes early bicycles, such as the Hobbyhorse and Boneshaker, and the problems associated with them. Inventors kept making one improvement after another to make bicycles better—up to the safe, comfortable models we have today. In "Biking to the Top," Greg LeMond set a number of goals for himself. Then he worked hard to get better and better, and he reached every one of his goals, finishing with three wins in the Tour de France.

23 Responses should reflect the coziness or homey atmosphere conveyed by "welcoming arms" and "soft."

25 Responses should indicate that Lillian is repeatedly surprised by (and not very polite about) Hattie's reactions to her new experiences. Examples include her trouble believing there aren't many cars where Hattie lives, her comment about Hattie not seeing a radiator before, and her amusement at Harriet's excitement about city sights. This suggests that Lillian has never considered that other people's lives might be different from hers. Lillian "didn't understand that Hattie was seeing a new world—strange, exciting, and a little bit scary."

30 Responses should be in paragraph form. The first paragraph introduces the main characters, the setting, and the plot element of this being Hattie's first trip to the city. Through details about the car, it reveals the time when the story takes place ("a brand-new 1915 Ford Model T") and sets the stage for Hattie's encounter with new gadgets. It also hints at the theme through the detail of Lillian's fashionable clothes not being very practical.

Writing Prompt

Refer to the scoring criteria in the Teacher Introduction.